Lander Rock Climbs

MW00639076

2011 Edition

A Climbers' Guide Featuring
Wild Iris, Sinks Canyon and More

Steve Bechtel

Volume 1 in the Cowboy Rock

series of climbing guides

elemental
climbing

Elemental Training Center

Lander, WY

DISCLAIMER

There are no warranties, whether expressed or implied, that this guidebook is accurate or that the information contained in it is reliable. Your use of this book indicates your assumption of the risk that it may contain errors and is an acknowledgment of your sole responsibility for your climbing safety.

elemental climbing

Elemental Training Center
134 Lincoln
Lander, WY 82520
or email to:
steve@elementaltraining.com

LANDER ROCK CLIMBS, 2011 Edition
A Climbers' Guide to Wild Iris, Sinks Canyon & More
by Steve Bechtel

ISBN 13: 978-1-4507-6874-0

15   14   13   12   11   1   2   3   4   5   6   7   8   9   10

Text © 2011 Steve Bechtel
Crag Photos © Steve Bechtel
Action Photos © As Indicated. Used by permission.
Maps, Illustrations & Layout © 2011 Joe Josephson.
All Rights Reserved.

Lander Sport Climbs, first edition, 2007. ISBN: 978-1-93309-03

Volume 1
"Cowboy Rock" Series of Wyoming Climbing Guides
Series Editor: Joe Josephson

Cover Photo: Kirk Billings climbing *Spurs Equal Velocity (12a)*. Photo © Bobby Model / M-11

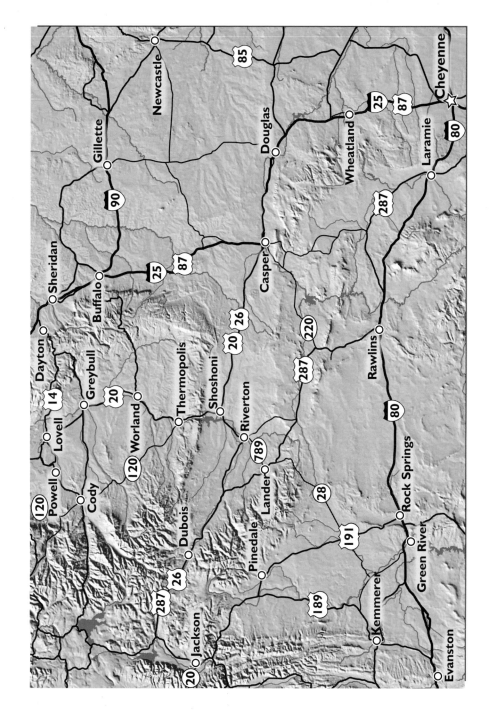

Steve Bechtel climbing *Bobcat Logic* **(12c).**
Photo © Bobby Model / M-11

DEDICATION

This book is dedicated to my friend, Todd Skinner. Todd loved climbing more than anyone I have ever known. He was determined. He was strong. He was kind. We shall not see his like again.

"You *must* believe."

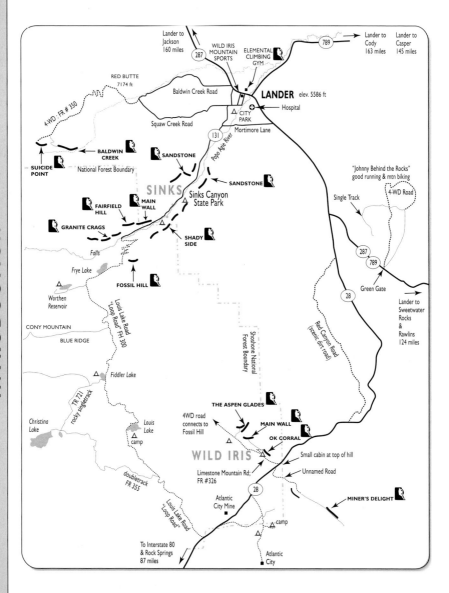

Lander to
Jackson
160 miles

287

WILD IRIS
MOUNTAIN
SPORTS

ELEMENTAL
CLIMBING
GYM

789

Lander to
Cody
163 miles

Lander to
Casper
145 miles

RED BUTTE
7174 ft

Baldwin Creek Road

4-WD: FR # 350

LANDER elev. 5586 ft

Hospital

CITY
PARK

Squaw Creek Road

Mortimore Lane

131

Pojo Agie River

"Johnny Behind the Rocks"
good running & mtn biking

BALDWIN
CREEK

SANDSTONE

4-WD Road

SUICIDE
POINT

National Forest Boundary

SANDSTONE

Single Track

SINKS

MAIN
WALL

Sinks Canyon
State Park

FAIRFIELD
HILL

287

GRANITE CRAGS

789

SHADY
SIDE

Green Gate

Falls

Frye Lake

28

FOSSIL HILL

Lander to
Sweetwater
Rocks
&
Rawlins
124 miles

Worthen
Reservoir

Louis Lake Road "Loop Road" FH 300

Red Canyon Road (scenic dirt road)

CONY MOUNTAIN

BLUE RIDGE

Shoshone National Forest Boundary

Fiddler Lake

TR 721 rocky singletrack

THE ASPEN GLADES

Christina
Lake

Louis
Lake

4WD road
connects to
Fossil Hill

MAIN WALL

Louis
Lake
camp

OK CORRAL

WILD IRIS

Small cabin at top of hill

doubletrack
FR 355

Limestone Mountain Rd;
FR #326

Unnamed Road

MINER'S DELIGHT

28

Atlantic
City Mine

"Louis Lake Road "Loop Road"

camp

To Interstate 80
& Rock Springs
87 miles

Atlantic
City

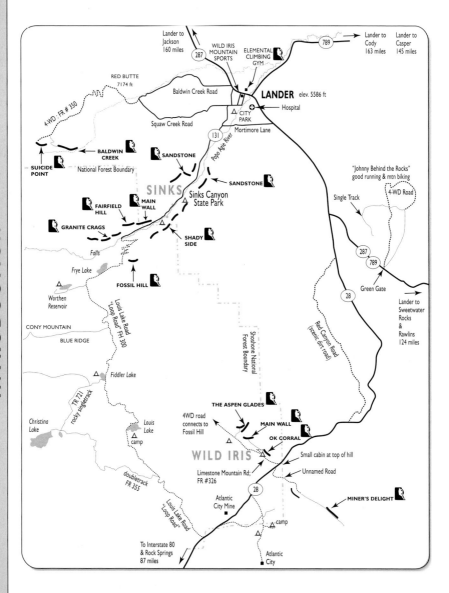 : Indicates cliffs described in this edition.

Map based on original by Daniel Miller. Used by Permission.

Welcome to Lander

Situated on the southeast flank of the Wind River Mountains, Lander, Wyoming is a rock climber's dream. Within one hour of town, there are close to two thousand rock climbs. Drive another hour, and you can add a thousand more. These climbs range from sandstone boulder problems, to one pitch limestone sport climbs, to grade V granite walls.

Best known for the sport routes at Wild Iris and Sinks Canyon, Lander offers decent bouldering, great granite climbing, and enough rest day activities to keep any climber happy for a pretty long time. An easy weekend trip from Salt Lake, Jackson, or Denver, the Lander area has much to offer the road-tripping climber.

Lander has grown into a climbers' town. Many full-time climbers moved here in the 90s, only to stay and become business owners, professionals, or full-time "has-beens." Buy a burger, cash a check, or get pulled over by a cop, and it's likely you'll be dealing with someone who came here to climb.

In the four years since we put together "Lander Sport Climbs," much has happened. The 50-plus years of climbing development in Lander continued at a good pace with nearly a hundred new climbs being done since 2007. The 5.14c grade was firmly established and a huge number of new moderates were opened. New crags were explored, old anchors were replaced, and climbers in the area continued an amicable and productive relationship with land managers.

With this edition, we update all the routes on the same nine cliffs covered in "Lander Sport Climbs," and have added details of climbs on two more granite crags in Sinks Canyon, the three "shady side" dolomite crags and five sandstone cliffs in the canyon. Also covered is the excellent Miner's Delight wall, which sits southeast of the Wild Iris area.

Future editions and new volumes in the "Cowboy Rock" series are an ongoing effort, with potential guides to cover Sweetwater and other great areas. For updates, including new route information for areas covered in this book, please visit www.elementalclimbing.com.

– Steve Bechtel, April 2011

Dedication photograph © Bobby Model.
Todd Skinner on *Comin' Home Curly* (14a), Sinks Canyon.
This photograph was made during Todd's redpoint ascent.

INTRODUCTION

Daniel Miller climbing *Blood Brother*, Sinks Canyon.
Photo © Ken Driese. December 2004.

Lander, Wyoming

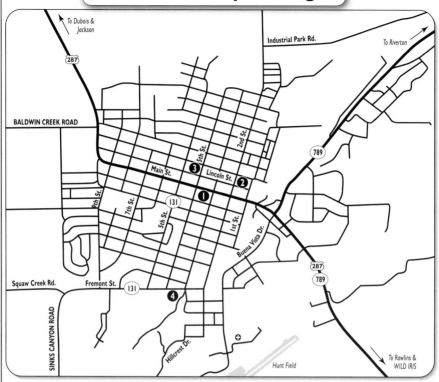

❶ : **WILD IRIS MOUNTAIN SPORTS** • 333 Main Street • 332-4541
❷ : **ELEMENTAL TRAINING CENTER** • 134 Lincoln Street • 332-0480
❸ : **NOLS & THE GULCH** • 502 Lincoln Street • 332-4784
❹ : **LANDER CITY PARK** • 405 Fremont Street • 332-4647

Climbing Gear and Gyms

❶ **Wild Iris Mountain Sports** is located at 333 Main Street. They have a wide range of gear and apparel. They also offer a large selection of guidebooks and maps of the Lander area and the Winds. 307-332-4541 : www.wildirisclimbing.com

❷ **Elemental Training Center** houses the local indoor climbing gym at 134 Lincoln Street. ETC offers day passes to a full fitness center and climbing gym. Showers are $5 and include use of a towel. 307-332-0480 : www.elementaltraining.com

❸ NOLS Rocky Mountain Branch and **The Gulch** are located at 502 Lincoln Street. NOLS Issue Room offers select gear and apparel while The Gulch provides a wide variety of bulk dried foods. The Gulch is a mandatory stop before heading into the Wind River Mountains. 307-332-4784 : www.nols.edu

Climbing Guides

Jackson Hole Mountain Guides (www.jhmg.com) and **Exum Mountain Guides** (www.exumguides.com), both based out of Jackson, WY, offer guiding services around Lander.

Water

❹ Water is available at the Lander City Park in the warmer months. Wild Iris Mountain Sports also has a water spigot outside their front door. Check inside before you fill up.

Paul Piana climbing *Cowboy King* (13b/c).
Photo © Bobby Model / M-11

Local Food and Beverages

Lander has a number of great restaurants with many styles and ethnicities to choose from.

Old Town coffee, hanging out, wireless, the usual. *205 Lincoln*

The Cowfish offers beef, seafood and great bowl food. *148 Main*

The Gannett Grill's patio welcomes you in the summertime to burgers and pizzas. This is THE place for climbers on the cheap. *126 Main*

The Lander Bar is Lander's most popular bar. Located right next door to the Gannett Grill. *126 Main*

El Sol de Mexico serves authentic Mexican food and effective margaritas. Take out is available. *453 Main*

Tony's Pizza has a menu full of pastas, salads and pizza. *637 W Main*

Asian Cuisine spices up Lander with a mixture of Thai, Indian and Cambodian cuisine. *140 N 7th*

Main Street Books serves books and coffee. Open late. *300 W Main*

Wildflour Bakery & Espresso serves bagels, sandwiches and coffee. *545 W Main*

China Garden serves authentic Chinese cuisine. *162 N 6th*

The Hitching Rack western steak house & salad bar. 983 *Hwy 789*

The Oxbow is your classic bacon & eggs breakfast joint. *170 Main*

Safeway and **Mr. D's Grocery Store**, are both located on Main Street. Mr. D's has a bakery and deli and both have **liquor stores**.

Other restaurants

Pizza Hut, *670 E Main*
The Summit, *260 Grand View Drive*
Subway, *960 W Main*
McDonalds, *235 McFarlane Drive*
Dairy Land Drive-In, *977 W Main*
The Bread Board, *1350 Main*
Apple Valley Market, *228 Main St*

Internet Access

Old Town Coffee : wireless, no computers
The Fremont County Library : computers
Wildflour Bakery : wireless, no computers

The City of Lander offers free camping in the City Park with a three day limit. There are toilets and water. See town map.

There are three campgrounds in Sinks Canyon. They first two have toilets and water. The third is a free campground with a pit toilet and no water.

Camping is also available at Wild Iris near the OK Corral. This is free camping with a 14 day limit. There is a pit toilet but no water.

Unimproved camping is also available near Baldwin Creek, Suicide Point and Fossil Hill. No services are available at these areas.

There is often a FIRE BAN during the summer months in and around Lander. Make sure you check before planning a campfire. Lander is also BEAR COUNTRY so please limit the BLTs in your pack and keep all camp food in hard containers inside your car.

FOSSIL HILL
elev. 9089 ft

INTRODUCTION

15

A Message from BARF

We all love sport clip anchors. Many of these graced the anchors of such popular climbs as *Action Candy* and *Wind River Rose*. But the use and abuse they take from visitors and locals alike has destroyed these in a very short time.

Even the toughest stainless steel rap anchors are suffering appalling wear, and the number of climbers visiting Sinks and the Wild Iris is growing every year. Each pair of sport clips cost almost $40. If we can't slow the rate of destruction, no one will be willing or able to replace them year after year.

And so we plead: Please, please, pretty please, top rope and lower on your own gear. Sport clips, rap rings, and springers alike are there for the sole purpose of safe cleaning and aren't designed for industrial-level top roping. When you get to any anchor, clip your draws to it and lower to the ground. Only the last climber in each party should ever climb on or lower off a rope through the anchors. It only takes a few seconds to clip in a couple draws; and it saves folks time, money, and anxiety.

Established in 1993, Lander's B.A.R.F. (Bolt Anchor Replacement Fund) is funded by local individuals, the International Climbers' Festival, the Wild Iris Gumball Machine, and occasional donations from traveling climbers. If you've never put money into a new route, now's your chance to help out. Wild Iris Mountain Sports on Main Street accepts donations to BARF which helps subsidize all our anchor replacement efforts. If you enjoy the climbing here, please consider helping maintain the safety and quality of the anchors around Lander.

Wild Iris Mountain Sports
333 Main Street
Lander, WY 82520

888-284-5968 : 307-332-4541
307-335-8923 fax

www.wildirisclimbing.com
wildiris@wildirisclimbing.com

Todd Skinner on *Wind Drinker*, **Suicide Point.**
Photo © Bobby Model / M-11

Access – Keeping Things Great

For over fifty years, climbers in Lander have enjoyed unrestricted access to crags and great support from local land managers. In fact, many of the people we work with in the three management agencies (BLM, Forest Service, and Sinks Canyon State Park) are climbers themselves.

Not only have these agencies helped develop and maintain trails, they've helped with climbers' camping areas, built pit toilets, and have provided anchor replacement hardware for popular climbs. Unfortunately, some climbers still abuse these relationships. Most recently, the difficulty has been in Sinks Canyon State Park.

State Park regulations require that all pets must be leashed while recreating on state park lands. The park is concerned with both the harassment of other climbers and the harassment of wildlife by climbers' unsupervised pets. (Ironically, the only time it's OK to have your dog off a leash is when you're using it to hunt and kill wildlife...). We all know that the dogs can be pretty overwhelming at the crags sometimes - it's a great idea to leash dogs in this congested area anyway. It's in our best interest to self-police on this one to avoid losing access.

There are also concerns about trail-cutting and new "braids" being made between climbs. It's imperative that we stick to the established trails and avoid shortcutting anywhere along the cliff. Although the state park has voiced the trail concern, this concern lies with the Forest Service and BLM, as well. Avoiding "new" trails or shortcuts on all three agencies' management areas is crucial to the long-term well-being of our privilege to climb here. We have a great relationship with the people at these agencies, but very simple and stupid actions can jeopardize our use of this area. When in doubt, stop and think.

Ellen Powick climbing *Nirvana* (13a).
Photo © David Anderson.

Greg Collins climbing *Wield the Scepter*, **Sinks Canyon.**
Photo © David Anderson.

Acknowledgments

Doing first ascents is thankless work. Anyone who thinks it's an ego trip just to get your name in a guidebook is a first-class fool. Not only is the work expensive, dirty, and dangerous, it's time-consuming.

There are literally hundreds of different first ascentionists that have been active on Lander's crags. Many of these people have done one or two new routes. A few people have done a dozen or so. But the real heroes are named Bob Branscomb, BJ Tilden, Paul Piana, Todd Skinner, Tom Rangitsch, and Greg Collins. These guys are not responsible for ten or even twenty new climbs each. Think fifty. Think 100. Or more.

Consider how much time it takes to do even one route, and you can thank your lucky stars that these men do what they do.

Other major pioneers include Kirk Billings, Frank Dusl, Ed Delong, Pete Absolon, Heidi Badaracco, Jim Ratz, Amy Skinner, Pete Delannoy, Leif Gasch, Mike Lindsey, Tom Hargis, Sue Miller, Dave Doll, Porter Jarrard, Rick Thompson, Gary Wilmot, Rick and Jeff Leafgreen, Bobby Model, and John Hennings. Each of these people, and many others, have given valuable time to our sport and this climbing area.

Maximum respect to my great friend Vance White, who has taken on the roles of Lander's climbing ambassador, first ascentionist, anchor repairman, mentor, historian, and trusted climbing partner. Vance's positive energy and enthusiasm for the sport make climbing here in Lander all the better.

Thanks especially to my wife Ellen who continues to stay strong and smart and loving, and to my two wonderful children. Thanks to you, my life is a dream.

And finally thanks To Joe Josephson, for once again wading into this project with me. Without Joe, this book would never happen.

– Steve Bechtel, April 2011

About the Author

Steve Bechtel began climbing in 1986 at Fremont Canyon, Wyoming. He likely would have quit the sport, but was not allowed to. He had been taken on as a belay slave for local legend Steve Petro in his epic quest to climb the now-legendary "Fiddler on the Roof," and quitting was not an option. In 1990, Steve was invited to climb at Sinks Canyon with his friend, Frank Dusl, who had rediscovered just how good the climbing was in his hometown. From that moment, Steve was enchanted with the wonderful climbing and the miles of beautiful, white stone in the hills outside Lander.

After finishing college at the University of Vedauwoo, Steve moved to Lander full time. Over the past twenty years, he has established over 200 new routes. These range from 25 foot sport routes to epic big wall free climbs in the greater ranges of the world. Between climbing days, he owns and operates Elemental Training Center (a climbing gym, fitness center and coaching business) with his wife, Ellen.

The Photographers

This edition would be just another ubiquitous climbing guide without the beautiful imagery and generosity of several additional Wyoming climbing pioneers—Bobby Model, Ken Driese, Mike Anderson, Mark Anderson and David Anderson. I have had the pleasure of knowing these guys for years, and feel lucky to have them as contributors to this area and to this work. The art these men create brings this area to life much more than any words I could possibly write.

For information on boulder problems around the Lander area, refer to Steve Bechtel's cleverly named Lander Bouldering; **available at Wild Iris Mountain Sports or Elemental Training Center in Lander**

Cover Photo from *Lander Sport Climbs*, 2007.
Climbing at Wild Iris. Photo © Bobby Model / M-11.

WILD IRIS OVERVIEW

The Limestone Mtn Road is usually inaccessible mid-November to mid-May due to snow.

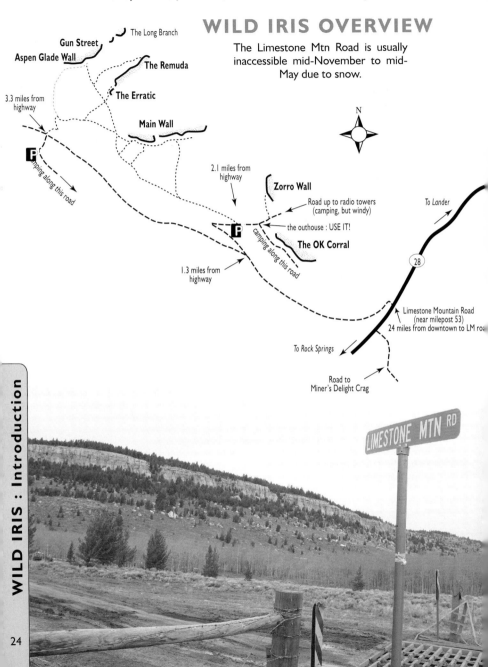

The Long Branch

Gun Street

Aspen Glade Wall

The Remuda

The Erratic

3.3 miles from highway

Main Wall

camping along this road

N

2.1 miles from highway

Zorro Wall

Road up to radio towers (camping, but windy)

the outhouse : USE IT!

The OK Corral

camping along this road

To Lander

28

1.3 miles from highway

Limestone Mountain Road (near milepost 53)
24 miles from downtown to LM road

To Rock Springs

Road to Miner's Delight Crag

LIMESTONE MTN RD

WILD IRIS

The Wild Iris area is one of the most beautiful rock climbing areas in America. Bone-white stone rising on a windswept ridge has yielded some of the fiercest short climbs anywhere. This area, set on the southeast flank of the Wind River Mountains, has been a magnet for climbers seeking to push their limits for almost 25 years.

Although there had been climbers exploring this area for a few years, Todd Skinner put this area on the map when he moved to nearby Atlantic City in 1990 and declared it the crag he had searched the world for. Soon after, Todd, his wife Amy, Jacob Valdez, Heidi Badaracco, Paul Piana, and a handful of others turned it into one of the most famous sport crags in the country.

Development of new routes has slowed since the early 1990s, but a few new routes get done each year. The crazy crowded days of the late 1990s are over, and Wild Iris is once again a quiet and idyllic crag most of the year. Some weekends there will only be one or two groups enjoying the now nearly 300 climbs spread across Limestone Mountain.

Wild Iris Crags

OK Corral & Zorro Wall : Page 26

Main Wall : Page 40

The Aspen Glades aka The Backside : Page 62

For this guide, I have divided the entire Wild Iris into three major areas: The OK Corral (including the OK Corral and Zorro Wall), The Main Wall (featuring everything from Rising From the Plains to the Cowboy Poetry Wall), and The Aspen Glades (which includes The Aspen Glade Wall, Gun Street, the walls of The Remuda, and The Erratic).

Some areas, such as the Longbranch, Carson City, and Lonesome Dove have not been included due to their remoteness or scarcity of established routes.

MAP LEFT: Wild Iris Overview. Area Overview on Page 8.

See each section for specific directions.

WILD IRIS : Introduction

Ellen Bechtel at Wild Iris.
Photo © Mike Lilygren.

WILD IRIS : OK Corral

The OK Corral is the shortest and least aesthetic dolomite cliff in the Lander area. It is also the most popular summertime crag due to the short approach and abundance of moderate routes.

The first sixteen routes described are at the Zorro section of the wall, a west facing cliff north of the main wall parking lot. These routes get afternoon sun.

The remainder of the routes are located on the cliff behind the outhouse, to the right of the large quarry. These routes face southwest, and are in the shade until about 10 a.m. in summer.

DRIVE TIME: 30 minutes from Lander

HIKE: 3 to 10 minutes flat walking

SUN EXPOSURE: A.M. shade only
Zorro, shade until Noon
OK Corral, shade until 10 a.m.

SEASON: Late Spring, Summer and Fall

LENGTH: 40 to 80 feet

OK CORRAL ROUTE COUNT by GRADE

<5.9 : 19 — 5.10 : 20 — 5.11 : 16 — 5.12 : 12 — 5.13 : 5

GETTING THERE (OK Corral & Main Wall)

To reach the Wild Iris Area, drive east out of Lander on Main Street. After about 24 miles (near milepost 53), take a right on the dirt Limestone Mountain Road (this sign tends to get stolen a lot, so look for a stop sign and cattle guard, which tend to be stolen less frequently). Take this road for 1.3 miles to a fork. The left fork goes to The Aspen Glade parking area, 2.0 miles up the road. To reach parking for the Main Wall and the OK Corral, take the right fork, switchback up the hill, and park on the left as you crest the ridge (0.8 miles past the fork). The Main Wall is to the northwest, and the OK Corral behind you to the southeast.

APPROACH (Zorro Wall)

The first sixteen routes described are at the Zorro section of the wall, a west-facing cliff to the north of the Main Wall parking lot. These routes get afternoon sun. (If you are looking toward the outhouse from the main parking area, this wall is downhill to your left.) The trail can be found by walking up the main road past the outhouse about 200 feet (not the OK Corral two-track), and looking for where it splits off downhill in a group of small trees. Follow this well-worn trail about 5 minutes to the cliff, which is visible for most of the approach.

OK Corral : Zorro Wall

Routes are listed right to left as they are encountered.

1. One Trick Sheep 11b
This climb is up and right of where the trail meets the wall. 60 feet

2. Burly Binkie 12b
Just above where the trail comes to the wall, this climb is burly from the get-go. 45 feet

3. Wet Wipe-a-Whet 10b
Face and slab left of *Burly Binkie*. 45 feet

4. Huggys Pull-up 8
Easier climb on face right of *Cirque du Suave*. 40 feet

5. Cirque du Suave 10b ★
This route begins in the corner, then moves out left and up a nice prow. 70 feet

6. Gaucho 10c ★★★
A low crux leads to challenging and sustained pulling above. Great climbing! 60 feet

7. Zorro 11d ★★★
Sustained difficulty up a beautiful face. This was the first route established at Wild Iris. 75 feet

8. Poposer Cowboy 12a ★★
A less-traveled cousin to *Zorro*, but a good climb nonetheless. Ain't over 'til it's over. 75 feet

9. Salsa for the Sole 12a

Up gully left of *Poposer Cowboy*, this is the rightmost route on the high wall. 60 feet

10. El Toro 12b

Center of the high face, through bulge. Very tricky. 60 feet

11. Friend or Faux 11c ★

Leftmost of the high routes, this is the best of the three. 50 feet

12. Ewenanimity 11b ★

This climb is on the leaning block just right of the tunnel. Fun, steep, juggy. 30 feet

13. The Guns I'll Never Own 11c ★

Also on the steep block, also fun. 35 feet

14. Chapito 7

Walk through the small tunnel to a short slab on the right. This is the right of two routes with chain hangers. 40 feet

15. Chico 8

Left of *Chapito*, another embarrassment. 40 feet

16. The Hangman 10d ★

About 50 feet left of the tunnel, this is a fun route. 40 feet

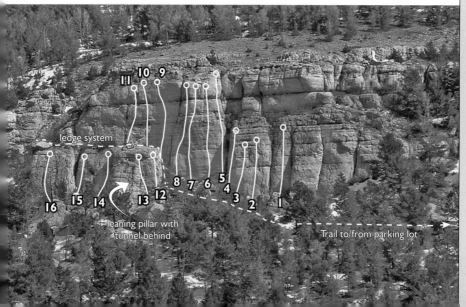

WILD IRIS : OK Corral

> **PARKING & APPROACH (OK Corral)**
>
> The cliff is approached by any of several trails leading through the woods from the rough road that passes along in front of the cliff. Due to congestion on this road, it is recommended that climbers park at the Main Wall parking lot and walk the extra 4-6 minutes it takes to get to the majority of routes.

Tribal War Wall

1. Western Front 11d
The less-popular of two routes that climb the vertical wall with a large bulge at the top. Begins in a crack feature. 65 feet

2. Tribal War 11b ★★
Parallel to *Western Front*. A really good route with a great headwall. You'll have to work to get there, though. 65 feet

3. Stirrup Trouble 12a
Tricky, thin route on the wall facing *Tribal War*. 45 feet

4. Stone Ranger 12b ★★
Good movement. A clean and pretty wall. 50 feet

5. Urban Cowboys 10c ★★
Fun climbing on good holds. 4 bolts, 40 feet

Poker-Face Alice Wall

The following routes are 25 yards east of *Urban Cowboys* and start on top of a series of big slabs. The *Poker-Face Alice* roof is hard to miss.

6. One-Eyed Jack 7 ★
Starts on big ledge system. Good climbing on short wall. 30 feet

7. Outlaws on the Run 6 ★★
On wall right of *One-Eyed Jack*, really good.

8. Poker-Face Alice 12b ★★
Climb 5.8 wall to a cold shut, then left and out roof. Obviously a little burly. 50 feet

9. Calamity Jane 13b ★
Break through the largest part of the *Poker-Face* roof. 50 feet

10. Three Charlies 7 ★
Acutally two slab routes about the same with 5 bolts. 40 feet

Due to the number of trees obscuring the routes it is almost impossible to get decent crag photos of the OK Corral cliff. In lieu of photos, use the overview topos and any relevant notes in the description to find your routes.

Routes are listed left to right as they are encountered.

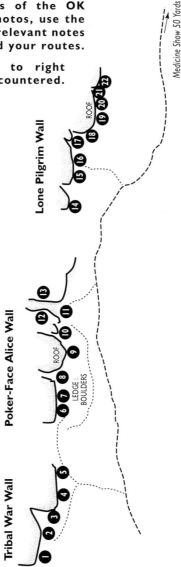

OK CORRAL : Left Side

The following three routes are in a small alcove down and east of the Poker Face Alice Roof.

11. High Plains Drifter 10c ★

The left route on the left wall in a small alcove. 4 bolts, 40 feet

12. Every Gun Sings Its Own Song 11b ★

Face just right of *High Plains Drifter*. 4 bolts, 40 feet

13. Don't Bring Your Guns to Town 12c ★★

Cool black wall with crimps and big moves. 5 bolts, 45 feet

Lone Pilgrim Wall ─────────────────────────

These routes are about 100 yards east of the previous climbs. This wall is easily identified by the very clean slab of *Lone Pilgrim*.

14. Battle for a Wounded Knee 10d ★★

Starts on ledges and moves past a big bush, then up left through a concave bulge. 40 feet

15. Only the Good Die Young 11b ★

Climb seam feature to small bulge. 7 bolts, 50 feet

16. Lone Pilgrim 11d ★

Clean slab with devious moves, gets steeper high. 6 bolts, 50 feet

17. Tongue Twister 5.11b *bolts chopped as of March 2011*

Begin climbing crack, then move onto thin prow. 50 feet

18. Black Box 11c *bolts chopped as of March 2011*

Climb up slab/flake system to ledges, then up chimney/stem to a high anchor. 65 feet

19. Under the Gun 12a or 13b/c ★

Good climbing up flakes and pockets to anchor well-below huge roof (12a). Continue up slab then out 10 foot roof. 70 feet

20. Heroes and Ghosts 12b ★

Bouldery and technical route, a stick clip is useful for the opening moves. Ends at a ledge below the big roof.

21. Hang 'em High 10c or 13d ★

This route climbs a 10c dihedral to a set of anchors, then out the right side of the high roof.

22. Drugstore Cowboy 11c

Climb rounded arête to the right of the roof wall. 5 bolts, 40 feet

The Medicine Show

The next two climbs are about 75 yards from *Drugstore Cowboy*, and begin in a small alcove/chimney. They are not visible from the trail.

23. Medicine Show 7 or 12a

Easy slab starting in chimney to high hard bulge. 45 feet to first anchor, 70 feet to second.

24. Spaghetti Western 10d

Steeper route in slot facing *Medicine Show*. 5 bolts, 40 feet

Blooming Rose Wall

The following climbs are all very close together on the Red as a Blooming Rose Wall. Routes 24 to 27 face generally west. Climbs 28 to 33 face south. These climbs are located just west of where the crag trail climbs steeply to a high point before dropping back down to *Claim Jumper*.

25. Iron Horse With a Twisted Heart 9 ★

A nice slab climb on the wall west of *Red As A Blooming Rose*. 3 bolts, 35 feet

26. Give My Love To Rose 12a ★★

Hardest route on the wall. High quality pulls between small pockets. 5 bolts, 40 feet

27. Red as a Blooming Rose 10d ★★

Thin start leads to big hold climbing at the top. 5 bolts, 40 feet

28. Roll in the Hay 11a ★

Technical climbing to corner system then up ledges above. 7 bolts, 45 feet

29. Stacked Deck 10b ★★

Starts on big jugs, getting tricky higher. 5 bolts, 45 feet

30. Matilda's Last Waltz 10d

Awkward climbing up prow, left of bushy crack. 5 bolts, 45 feet

31. Cowboys are my Only Weakness 11a

Rounded prow. 4 bolts, 40 feet

32. Aces and Eights 10b ★

Starts above gnarled tree, up seams and underclings. 4 bolts, 50 feet

33. Never Sit With Your Back to the Door 10b ★★

Tricky long moves up to a small ledge. 4 bolts, 45 feet

34. Brown Dirt Cowgirl 10a ★★

Nice wall just left of corner. 3 bolts, 40 feet

35. Phat Phinger Phrenzy 8 ★

Climb up a strange corner feature. Fun. 6 bolts, 50 feet

36. Dogfight at the OK Corral 11d

Another rounded and tricky prow climb. 5 bolts, 45 feet

Claim Jumper Wall ─────────────────────

These four climbs are just over the small hill east of *Dogfight*.

37. Claim Jumper 10c ★★★

Right-leaning lieback seam to juggy headwall. 6 bolts, 50 feet

38. Annie Get Your Drill 9 ★

Follow a crack feature on the prow then up face holds above. 6 bolts, 50 feet

39. Miner's Dee-Light 11d ★

Bouldery low moves to a nice rest then some more challenge. 5 bolts, 45 feet

40. Greenhorns in Velvet 7 ★

Very popular route up a nice clean slab. 50 feet

Winchester Wall ─────────────────────

The three Winchester routes are on a nice long wall behind a large pine tree about 100 feet right of *Greenhorns in Velvet*.

41. Sharps 50 11a *bolts chopped as of March 2011*

Up slab left of *Winchester Pump*, and then up steep wall to low anchor. 50 feet

42. Winchester Pump 11a ★★

Climb center of slab, then up bulging wall on good moves. 60 feet

43. Red Ryder 10a ★★★

Follows a flake up the right slide of slab, then up nice headwall. 60 feet

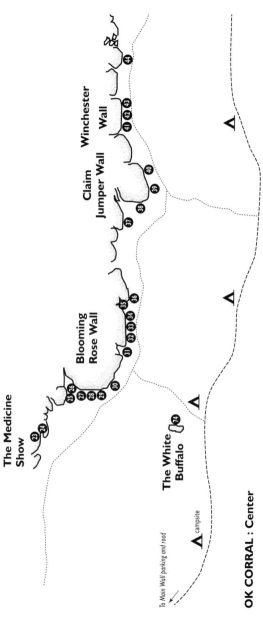

The Medicine Show

Blooming Rose Wall

Claim Jumper Wall

Winchester Wall

The White Buffalo

To Main Wall parking and road

△ campsite

OK CORRAL : Center

Saddle Tramp Wall ——————————————

After *Red Ryder*, the trail meanders away from the cliff, and the routes are spaced out about 100 feet apart. The trail comes back close to the cliff at the overhanging *Saddle Tramp*.

44. Jabba the Hut 10a
Up small buttress to high long chain anchor. 50 feet

45. 30 Seconds on Fremont Street 11b ★
Bouldery climbing up short clean wall. 35 feet

46. Back in the Saddle 10c
Somewhat tricky route up west-facing wall. 40 feet

47. Saddled Dreams 11c ★★
Start on *Saddle Tramp*, moving up and left through a small roof. Devious. 40 feet

48. The Saddle Tramp 12a ★
Up bulge on undercuts and thin pockets. 40 feet

49. Whips, Chaps, and Chains 11d ★★
Rightward trending route up pockets and edges through bulge. 40 feet

Diamond Wall ——————————————

50. Boob Loob 10a ★ *bolts chopped as of March 2011*
Climbs rounded bear-hug prow and high up wall above. 65 feet

51. Diamonds and Rain 11d ★★
Clean, vertical white face with cold shut anchors. 4 bolts, 45 feet

52. Scary Canary 8 *bolts chopped as of March 2011*
Runout face climbing right of crack. A lame attempt at "bold" climbing. 50 feet

53. When the Man Comes Around 12c ★★
Bouldery short face with four bolts. 35 feet

54. Bull of the West 8
Short route with four bolts to anchor below small tree. 40 feet

55. Guns of Diablo 8
Adjacent short route. 40 feet

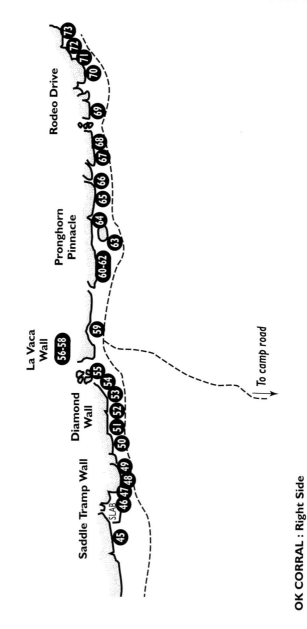

Rodeo Drive

Pronghorn Pinnacle

La Vaca Wall

Diamond Wall

Saddle Tramp Wall

To camp road

OK CORRAL : Right Side

La Vaca Wall ——————————————

56. Sugarfoot 10c
Powerful little route that starts behind a big flake.

57. Slave 8
Face behind flake. 35 feet

58. "R" is for Redneck 7
Slab climb that starts just right of flake, and left of a big crack. 35 feet

59. La Vaca Peligrosa 8 ★★
Nice climb right of large crack. 40 feet

Pronghorn Pinnacle ——————————————

The following three climbs are on a nice wall behind a group of large trees. These are just west of the obvious tiny "Pronghorn Pinnacle". Two more routes are found on the pinnacle itself.

60. Britchen Strap 9
Nice route with thin start. 45 feet

61. Licorice Stick 8 ★
Again, a hard start to easier rock above. 45 feet

62. Saddle Up 9 ★
Hardest of the three. 45 feet

63. Pronghorn Pinnacle 8
The west face of the small "Pronghorn Pinnacle" that sits in front of the cliff. 3 bolts. 20 feet

64. Nouveau Western 10a
This climb takes an arête on the east side of the pinnacle. 25 feet

These routes are on the nice walls past the pinnacle. This quiet area is worth a visit.

65. The Hanging Tree 9 ★

Slab climb 50 feet right of *Pronghorn Pinnacle*, behind a few large pines. 45 feet

66. Ticks for Chicks 8 ★★

Dark slab left of chimney feature, faces southeast. 4 bolts, 40 feet

67. Ride Me Cowgirl 10b

AKA *Route 64*. Face just right of prow and left of junk rock. 4 bolts, 40 feet

68. Dirty Sally 10c

This climb takes the face right of *Ride Me Cowgirl*.

69. The Man From Laramie 10c ★

This route climbs a rounded prow feature past several horizontals, ending at anchors below a blocky bulge. 55 feet

70. Rodeo Drive 11c

Climb grey slab 15 feet right of rounded white prows. 4bolts, 40 feet

71. The Solace of Bolted Faces 12a ★★

Climb slab with seams just left of a crack with big bushes in it. 45 feet

72. John Wayne 13b ★★

Reachy, technical, and bouldery have all been used to describe this clean line.

73. Drinking Dry Clouds 12c ★

A four bolt route up a pretty little bulge at the very right end of the cliff band. 35 feet

The White Buffalo

74. The White Buffalo V11 or 13d ★

This is a short and savage route on a beautiful clean boulder near the third campsite on the left. It is on an east-facing wall and is visible from the camp road.

For more bouldering in the Lander area, refer to Steve Bechtel's cleverly named *Lander Bouldering;* **available at Wild Iris Mountain Sports.**

This is the crag that started it all. It's not the first crag that was developed in the area, nor does it have the greatest number of routes, but it's the one that put Lander on the map. The routes are short and powerful affairs and the perfect white stone is magic to climb on. Each section of this cliff has its own distinct character; from the beautifully steep Rodeo Wave, to the "thug" bulges of the Hot Tamale, to the clean verticality of Cowboy Poetry.

Expect warm days in the summer, and perfect cool conditions all fall. Take care in hiking the ridge back to the parking lot during afternoon thunderstorms. This hike is very exposed to the elements. It's best to just wait out these short storms and hike out a few minutes later than you'd planned.

DRIVE TIME: 30 minutes from Lander

HIKE: 20 to 25 minutes flat

SUN EXPOSURE: Sunny from dawn until 7 p.m.

SEASON: Late Spring, Summer and Fall

LENGTH: 25 to 80 feet

MAIN WALL ROUTE COUNT by GRADE

<5.9 : 5 — 5.10 : 28 — 5.11 : 22 — 5.12 : 27 — 5.13 : 11 — 5.14 : 6

BJ Tilden surfing the "wave"
on *Atomic Stetson* (13c).
Photo © Mark Anderson.

GETTING THERE (Main Wall & OK Corral)

To reach the Wild Iris Area, drive east out of Lander on Main Street. After about 24 miles (near milepost 53), take a right on the dirt Limestone Mountain Road (this sign tends to get stolen a lot, so look for a stop sign and cattle guard, which tend to be stolen less frequently). Take this road for 1.3 miles to a fork. The left fork goes to The Aspen Glade parking area, 2.0 miles up the road. To reach parking for the Main Wall and the OK Corral, take the right fork, switchback up the hill, and park on the left as you crest the ridge (0.8 miles past the fork). The Main Wall is to the northwest, and is clearly visible from the parking lot.

WILD IRIS : Main Wall

Routes are listed left to right as they are encountered.

WILD IRIS : Main Wall

Rising from the Plains & Chaps Wall : **A**
Rodeo Wave Wall : **B**
Wild Horses Wall : **C**
Hot Tamale Wall : **D**
Five Ten Wall : **E**
Rode Hard Wall : **F**
Cowboy Poetry Wall : **G**

Bill Hickok

Rising from the Plains

1. Rising From The Plains 12b ★★
This is the leftmost (west) route on the Wild Iris Main Wall. Climb a vertical white wall to a grey streak that goes through a short bulge. 40 feet

2. Cowboy Killer 12b/c ★★
Follow a zigzag bolt line up through the right side of the bulge. 40 feet

3. Project
Anchors only. Up slab to flake. 40 feet

4. A Slug of the Old What-For 13d ★
Begin up *Adi-Goddang-Yos*, then track left across the belly of the big bulge. 35 feet

5. Adi-Goddang-Yos 13c
Begin in a right-facing corner, then up and right through a very steep bulge to a baffling crux.

6. Whip and Spur 14b ★★
This links *You Ain't Bill Hickok* to *A Slug of Old What-For*.

7. You Ain't Bill Hickok 14a
Straight out the big belly. 45 feet

8. Last Man Standing 13b ★★
Climb up steep belly (using first bolt of *Hickok*) to nice climbing on overhanging wall. 45 feet

9. Pocket Derringer 11a
Harder start through low bulge leads to long moves up slab. 50 feet

10. Crazy Hörst 12b
Six feet right of *Pocket Derringer*, this technical and devious route follows a grey streak past six bolts. 50 feet

11. Project High bolt only.

12. The Lord Loves a Hangin' 13a
Behind a big tree, climb up a seam feature past six bolts to a cold shut anchor. 50 feet

13. Chaps 12d
Follows a black streak past four bolts. 45 feet

14. Horsewhipped and Hogtied 12d ★★
Climb left and up seam to very crimpy crux. 6 bolts, 50 feet

15. Très Hombres 13a ★
Slightly overhanging on slightly terrible holds. Anchor near a small pine. 5 bolts, 40 feet

Rodeo Wave Wall ─────────────────────

16. The Ranch 12d

Steep line tucked between slab and wave. 35 feet

17. Ground From Upside Down 12d ★★★

Tucked in between the slab and the rodeo wave. Boulder it. Amazing. 65 feet

18. Bobcat Logic 12c ★★★

Climb big holds on the left-most line off the slab. Most climbers clip the first bolt of *Cow Reggae* to keep the rope out of the way. 35 feet

19. Bob Marley 12b ★★

This hybrid climb is the easiest outing at the Rodeo Wave. Start *Bobcat Logic*, move right at half-height and finish on *Cow Reggae*.

20. Cow Reggae 13b ★★

A popular and fun route, the straight up line just right of *Bobcat Logic*. 4 bolts, 35 feet

21. Babalouie 12c ★★

Takes the first two bolts of *Cow Reggae*, then moves right to finish the final two of *Atomic Stetson*. 4 bolts, 35 feet

22. Atomic Stetson 13c ★★

This is the third straight up line from the left. 40 feet

23. Atomic Cow 13d ★★

Starts as *Atomic Stetson*, then traverses left onto *Cow Reggae* where *Babalouie* goes right. Slightly harder than *Atomic Stetson*. 45 feet

24. Rodeo Free Europe 14a ★★

This route goes up the longest part of the wave. The hardest of the straight up lines. 50 feet

25. Genetic Drifter 14c

Starts on *Rodeo Free Europe*, drifts left on *Atomic Stetson*, then finishes *Cow Reggae*. 55 feet

26. High Way 14b

This may have been the original first ascent line by J.C. Basically, traverse left one bolt higher than *Genetic Drifter*. 55 feet

27. Rodeo Active 14a? ★

The right-most line. A very hard move (now even harder since a hold broke) leads to relatively easy climbing above. 45 feet

Wild Horses Wall

28. Project NFR

Longstanding project.

29. Two Kinds of Justice 12b ★★

Begins behind a large blocky formation. Popular, with long and bouldery moves all the way. 40 feet

30. Gored By Inosine 12d ★

A pretty wall with very long moves. Look for a big hueco to identify this climb. 40 feet

31. In Todd We Trust 11d ★

Just right of *Gored by Inosine*. Dihedral climb with a black streak, features and exit crux. 45 feet

32. Limestone Cowboy 12a ★

Behind the big pine; start with a small overhang; climb up nice rock. 45 feet

33. Hip Boot Romance 10d

A little bit strange, but a decent climb. 45 feet

34. Pronghorn Love 11d

Awkward moves lead up a pretty wall. 50 feet

35. The Prospect 10d ★★

Starts in left-facing corner, then up big pockets. 50 feet

36. The Devil Wears Spurs 10d ★★

Famous and popular, this route is getting slick! Start with big pockets near "double" pine tree. 50 feet

37. Posse On My Tail 11d ★

Bouldery climbing leads to a tricky wall above. 50 feet

38. Wild Horses 11b

Start near small corner/chimney, then up lower angled wall above. 50 feet

39. Jackalope and Boomslang 10a

Climbs the low-angle wall right of the main Wild Horses Wall. 45 feet

Mark Anderson climbing *Two Kinds of Justice* **(12b).**
Photo © Mike Anderson.

40. In God's Country 12b

Up wall through small bulges and awkward sequences. A little sharp, but takes a pretty line. This is the leftmost route on the Hot Tamale Wall. 45 feet

41. Ruby Shooter 12b ★★

Popular route with great movement. 55 feet

42. Hot Tamale Baby 11d ★★★

Also popular, with great movement. Begin in a little left-facing corner leading to rounded prow. Wanders a bit at top. 60 feet

43. Hey, Mr. Vaquero 12c ★★

Follows a grey streak. Breaks through the left side of the low bulge on long moves, then up a tricky headwall. 70 feet

44. Mexican Rodeo 12d ★★

The hardest of the bulges followed by the hardest headwall. There is a large pocket right at first bolt. 70 feet

45. Charro 12b ★★★

Big moves on big holds, then up tricky slab and past small roof. Look for underclings to identify the start. 75 feet

46. Caballero Del Norté 11d ★

Fun hard start to thin moves high. 50 feet

47. Windy City 9 ★★

Follow a corner/crack system, then climb right to anchors at the top. 50 feet

48. Popo Agie Pocket Pool 10a ★

This route is left of a big dead tree right next to the wall. Good climbing up to share anchors with *Windy City*. 50 feet

49. Osita 11a ★★
Hard move low to easier slab above. Just right of dead tree. 5 bolts, 45 feet

50. Digital Stimulation 10c
Big pockets into tricky seam. Faces east and starts off small ledge. 4 bolts, 40 feet

51. The Shootist 10a ★
Good pockets up clean wall. 5 bolts, 40 feet

52. Wind River Rose 9 ★★
Nice slab climbing up rounded prow. 5 bolts, 45 feet

53. Ryobi Jr. 10b ★

Starts on ledge system left of the Five Ten Wall. Face left of tree. 4 bolts, 40 feet

54. Ryobi Rustler 10d

From ledge system, climb right of tree up orange streak. 5 bolts, 40 feet

55. Ryobi Wrangler 11a ★

Climb off right side of ledge system, up black streak. 4 bolts, 40 feet

56. Ryobi Ranger 10a ★★

The leftmost route on the Five Ten Wall itself. Climbs up to big pockets, then through some reachy moves before easing up at the top. 5 bolts, 50 feet

57. Indian Country 10b ★★

Most climbers start on the small ledge to the right, then move up and left to good pockets. 4 bolts, 50 feet

58. Dynamitic 7 ★

Up left-facing corner about 10 feet left of the large "Stonehenge" rock that sits in front of the wall. 5 bolts, 45 feet

59. Sacagawea 10b

Starts behind left side of "Stonehenge" rock. Thin hard moves. 3 bolts, 45 feet

60. Pistol Pete 10d

Starts behind right side of "Stonehenge" rock. Thin hard moves. 4 bolts, 45 feet

61. Wild Horses Keep Dragging Me Away 10c ★

Another hard slabby face. 5 bolts, 45 feet

62. You Picked a Fine Climb to Lead Me, Lucille 9 ★

Surprisingly long moves up a streak lead to easier climbing above. Ends near a small pine tree. 40 feet

63. Latex Cowboy 10b ★★

Ten feet left of bushy crack. Steeper climbing on good pockets. (no photo) 5 bolts, 40 feet

64. T & T 10c ★

Clean white wall 15 feet left of chockstone chimney. (no photo) 5 bolts, 40 feet

WILD IRIS : Main Wall

Five Ten Wall
100 feet

65. Pistols and Gri Gris 11a

These routes are 50 to 60 feet right of the main Five Ten Wall. Hard moves low to lower-angle wall above. 4 bolts, 45 feet

66. War Paint 11b

Very bouldery low moves, to easier climbing above. Shares anchors with *Pistols and Gri Gris*. 4 bolts, 45 feet

67. "Dances With Wolves" & "Wind in His Hair" 7 TR

Up the gully right of *War Paint*. 20 foot clean wall.

Dave Body climbing *Wind & Rattlesnakes* **(12a).**
Photo © Bobby Model / M-11

Rode Hard Wall

68. Project Jones on the Jukebox
This project takes the unlikely line out the bottom of a huge block leaning against the left end of the *Rode Hard* roof.

69. Full Circle 13a ★★
Shares start with *Copenhagen*, then breaks left and out a roof.

70. Copenhagen Angel 13b ★
Up white wall to climb through the biggest part of the roof. Face up to roof is 5.11. 7 bolts, 60 feet

71. Phony Express 12b ★
Starts same as *Rode Hard*, moves left on good pockets through roof. 7 bolts, 60 feet

72. Rode Hard and Put Up Wet 12c ★★
Climb clean slab starting on left side of flake/crack, heading toward "hueco" in the roof. Devious sequence through center of roof. This was the first route at the Main Wall. 6 bolts, 55 feet

73. Nine Horse Johnson 11c ★★
Up flake to vertical wall with good pockets. Out roof on jugs and stems. 6 bolts, 55 feet

74. Wind and Rattlesnakes 12a ★★★
Up nice prow, great continuous climbing. 5 bolts, 50 feet

WILD IRIS : Main Wall

57

75. Tomahawk Slam 12a ★
Crack/jug climbing to stinger move, then easier to top. 6 bolts, 50 feet

76. Easy Ridin' 10d ★★★
Great climbing up flakes to small bulge and up fun wall. 8 bolts, 55 feet

77. Arizona Cowgirl 11c ★★
Thin moves to easier wall above. This is the leftmost climb on the *Buckskin Billy* Slab. 7 bolts, 50 feet

78. Cowboy Joe 10c ★
A bulge low leads to easier climbing high. 50 feet

79. Buckskin Billy 10a ★
Tricky through the bulge, then great moves up to anchor. 45 feet

80. Hired Guns 11d
Around right of the *Buckskin Billy* slab, this route is a thin and tricky pursuit. 4 bolts, 40 feet

81. Unknown 10b ★
Climbs the short clean wall 100 feet right of Hired Guns.

82. Unknown 10d
This dirty, poor, sharp route takes a layback crack and flake just right of the previous climb. The climbing equivalent of "The Last Airbender."

Lauren Edwards climbing *Tomahawk Slam* (12a).
Photo © David Anderson.

83. Gumby 11a

Fifteen feet left of *Latex*. Climb slab then bulge.

84. The Devil Wears Latex 10c ★★

This short route is left of the main Cowboy Poetry Wall, good pockets and fun moves. 5 bolts, 45 feet

85. Even Cowgirls Get The Blues 11a

Up bulgy wall, sneaks through bulges on right side. 60 feet

86. Testosterone Alfresco 10d ★

Shares the start of *Sleeping Thunder*, moving left after 25 feet. Up prow and over a small bulge. 55 feet

87. Sleeping Thunder 12a ★

Good climbing up vertical wall to a crux high, usually marked by a bail biner. 65 feet

88. Cowboy Poetry 11b/12a ★★★

P1 Up slab to scoop, then tricky long moves to anchor at horizontal (11b). 7 bolts, 50 feet

P2 From horizontal clip bolt up and right, then fight through bulges to upper anchor. 3 bolts, 30 feet

89. Cowboy Gibberish 11b *bolts chopped as March 2011*

Left variation finish of *Cowboy Poetry*. Easier climbing into corner above. 65 feet

90. Take Your Hat Off 10b ★★★

Hard start to jug climbing, ending at anchor below bulge. 6 bolts, 50 feet

91. Boy 13a ★

Continue up headwall above *Take Your Hat Off*. 4 bolts, 35 feet

92. Buffalo Soldier 10b ★

Edgy climbing starting on flake. 5 bolts, 45 feet

93. Charlie Drew That Spinnin' Bull 12c ★

Continues through bulges above *Buffalo Soldier*.

WILD IRIS : Main Wall

94. Cowboys Don't Shoot Straight 10c ★

Up black streak below the obvious cracks in the upper bulge. 5 bolts, 50 feet. The hangers may be missing.

95. Pokey 5.11a *bolts chopped as of March 2011*

Climb the crack system above *Cowboys Don't Shoot Straight*. 65 feet

96. Ambush in the Night 11a ★

Tricky thin moves just left of small pine against the wall. 5 bolts, 45 feet

97. Riata Man 12c ★

Up bulging wall with obvious big pockets above *Ambush in the Night*. 4 bolts, 40 feet

98. Princess and the Playmate 10c ★★

First route right of small pine, low bulge to slab. 6 bolts, 50 feet

WILD IRIS : Main Wall

99. Cherokee With a Crewcut 11a ★

Climb up seam and through steep wall above with black streak. 5 bolts, 50 feet

100. Slapping Leather 11c

Start in seam then to right and steeper terrain. 5 bolts, 60 feet

101. Concrete Cowboys 10c

Wanders up and left, then back right to anchor. 5 bolts, 45 feet

102. Honed on the Range 11c ★★

Tricky route behind large pine tree. 6 bolts, 50 feet

103. Hand-Tooled Saddle 11c

On wall 100 feet right of *Honed*, up seams in steep wall.

104. Bucky Goldstein 12b

Thin face.

Cowboy Poetry Wall

Dave Body climbing *Bronc Twister* **(13a).**
Photo © **Bobby Model** / **M-11**

WILD IRIS : The Aspen Glades

The Aspen Glades (aka The Backside) area of Wild Iris is home to some of the best climbs anywhere. The valley behind the Main Wall includes the cliffs of The Aspen Glade, Remuda, and The Erratic. The Aspen Glade Wall features some of the cleanest stone at Wild Iris. This wall faces southeast and is pleasant late into the fall. For summer climbing, the walls of The Remuda and Erratic offer shade most of the day. Be warned, though, that the routes on these walls tend to be very difficult – this is not a beginner's crag. Also in this little valley are the crags known as The Longbranch and Lonesome Dove. Because of their remoteness and lack of route density, they will not be covered in this edition.

DRIVE TIME: 35 minutes from Lander

HIKE: 30 to 40 minutes up and down hills

SUN EXPOSURE: Aspen Glade – sunny until 4 p.m. most of the year
Remuda & Erratic – shade most of the day

SEASON: Late Spring, Summer and Fall

LENGTH: 40 to 90 feet

ROUTE COUNT by GRADE (Aspen Glades, Erratic, Remuda)

5.10 : 13 — 5.11 : 19 — 5.12 : 15 — 5.13 : 5 — 5.14 : 2

GETTING THERE & PARKING (The Aspen Glades)

To reach The Aspen Glades, drive east out of town on Main Street. After about 25 miles, take a right on the dirt Limestone Mountain Road (this sign tends to get stolen a lot, so look for a stop sign and cattle guard, which tend to be stolen less frequently). Take this road for 1.3 miles to a fork. The Main Wall parking and the OK corral are up the right fork. To get to The Aspen Glades, stay left at the fork. Take this road about 2 miles until you begin to enter a wooded area. Look for parking on the left, near a less-traveled dirt road. From this parking area, walk back up Limestone Mountain Road about 50 yards, and take a trail through the woods to the left (north).

Aspen Glade Wall

APPROACH (The Aspen Glades aka The Backside)

The hike takes you out of the woods and switchbacks to the crest of the ridge. From here, you can see the cliffs. Walk roughly east on a trail that is occasionally a two track, following cairns. The trail drops down into a little valley and eventually to a 4-way intersection near some large dead trees. To reach the Aspen Glade, go left at this intersection. This should be really obvious, as there is a big cliff to your left with an aspen glade in front of it. To reach The Remuda, also go left, but bear right before reaching The Aspen Glade wall (see map below). The Erratic is reached by going straight at the intersection. You really can't miss it. Going right leads you uphill and to the very west end (Rising From the Plains) of the Main Wall.

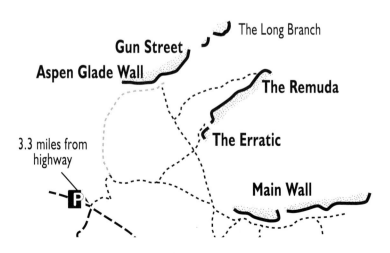

The Long Branch

Gun Street

Aspen Glade Wall

The Remuda

The Erratic

3.3 miles from highway

Main Wall

Gun Street Area

9 10 11 19 27

Routes are listed left to right

The Climbs

Climbs on The Aspen Glade Wall are described left to right. This wall can be approached via a trail that comes in along the cliff from the west to route #1, or by following the trail in from the 4-way intersection at the dead trees. If this approach is used, you reach the cliff at route #16.

1. Ambuscado 11d ★★

Follows very steep line on back of huge, leaning detached slab. 100 feet left of *Spurs* wall. 4 bolts, 35 feet

2. Night-Flying Woman 10d ★★

Starts right of bushy gully, then up great rock on good holds. 5 bolts, 40 feet

3. Buffalo Skull 11d ★

Good climbing. Used to be weird at top, but new anchor placement is better. 8 bolts, 70 feet

4. Straight Outta Hudson 12c ★★

Bouldery through roof at bottom, up slab, then through biggest part of upper roof. 9 bolts, 70 feet

5. Spurs Equal Velocity 12a ★★

Climb through right side of low roof (5.11), then up slab to six foot roof. 70 feet

6. Mutt Ridin' Monkey 10d

A bit sharp, but pretty fun climbing. 60 feet

7. Californios 11c

Starts just left of small corner, up steep face to share anchors with *Mutt Ridin' Monkey*. 60 feet

8. Hillbilly Hoedown 12a

On large block downhill and right of *Spur Equal Velocity* wall. See photo page 62. Steep face with wandering bolts. 40 feet

9. Prime Bovine Arête 11c

On the buttress halfway between *Spurs* and *Gun Street*, up a hourglass prow. See photo page 63. 5 bolts, 50 feet

10. Lonesome Cowboy 10c ★

Good climbing, but really short. See photo page 63. 3 bolts, 30 feet

WILD IRIS : Aspen Glades

11. Miss Yvonne Rode the Horse 11b ★
Four bolts to clip anchors. See photo page 63. 30 feet

12. Young Guns 10d ★
The black and gold wall left of *Little Buckaroo*.

13. Little Buckaroo 11b ★★★
Really fun. Three bolts to clip anchors. On west-facing wall. 25 feet

14. Bovine Intervention 10d ★
Just right of *Little Buckaroo* pillar, long moves up vertical wall to short crux. 6 bolts, 50 feet

15. Lonely are the Brave 11a ★★
Up steep wall with good holds to crux finish. 5 bolts, 45 feet

16. Don't Paint Your Wagon 12a ★★
Good pockets and good moves. Tricky. 5 bolts, 45 feet

17. Branded 12a
Up center of wall, follows flakes and small pockets. 5 bolts, 45 feet

18. Butch Pocket and the Sundance Pump 12a ★★★
Nice moves on big holds up seam feature to an attention-getting crux. 6 bolts, 50 feet

19. Gun Street Girl 12b ★★★

Good climbing up sinker pockets to high crux. 7 bolts, 50 feet

20. Sweet Tart of the Rodeo 10d

Powerful moves up short overhanging face to lower angle top. 7 bolts, 45 feet

21. Dirt Bag 11d ★

Begins atop orange-lichened flake. Ascend though bulges, trending left. Strange position, but good moves. 8 bolts, 50 feet

22. Sweating Bullets 10a

Up left side of slabby wall. 5 bolts, 45 feet

23. Sweaty Bully 10b ★★

Good climbing up steep rock to slab. 6 bolts, 50 feet

24. Whiskey Toast 11d

Hard long moves. A bit sporty toward the top. 5 bolts, 50 feet

25. Fist Full of Quickdraws 11d ★★

Good moves on nice rock. 6 bolts to chain anchor. 50 feet

26. The Quick and the Dead 11d ★

Tricky climbing on sloping pockets. Good route. 6 bolts, 50 feet

27. Bronc Twister 13a ★★

Up dancy slab to two-tiered roof. 5.12+ though first roof, move left, then the business. 9 bolts, 75 feet

28. Cowboy King 13b/c ★★★

Shares start with *Bronc Twister*. After first roof crux, breaks right where BT breaks left. 9 bolts, 75 feet

29. American Beauty 12b ★★★

Hard move low, then up to long roof moves. 9 bolts, 75 feet

30. Jolly Rancher 12c ★

Very tricky low face to easier climbing at top. 70 feet

31. Choke Cherry Eyes 12a ★★

Continuous fun moves up vertical wall then through bulge at top. 70 feet

This cliff is actually a huge tilted boulder. It has the highest concentration of hard moves in the area, and is an absolutely beautiful piece of stone. One of the first and best 5.14s in America, *Throwin' the Houlihan* has had many ascents and is considered a gold-standard 14a.

To help orient yourself to The Erratic and The Remuda, see Aspen Glades Map on Page 64.

APPROACH (The Erratic)

Routes are described right to left, as they are encountered along the trail. Routes 1-5 are on the Erratic itself, routes 6-11 are another 150 yards downhill and east on a nice buttress.

1. Throwin' the Houlihan 14a ★★★

Step off boulder then up long moves on small pockets. The direct start boulder problem has been climbed, raising the route difficulty slightly. 50 feet

2. Project Moonshine

Up prow/seam to very unlikely moves. 50 feet

3. Ghost Moon 13d

Starts first two bolts of *Moonshine*, then left to finish on *Heart Full of Ghosts*. 50 feet

4. Heart Full of Ghosts 14a ★★

Takes the line just left of a prow on monos and long moves. 50 feet

5. When I Was a Young Girl, I Had Me a Cowboy 13a ★★

Up steep left side of the *Erratic* with many possible sequences. 45 feet

6. Wutang 11b

Just right of *Wotai*, has a slab crux low. Tricky. 45 feet

7. Wotai 10d ★★★

Start in crack, then move right onto nice face with a small roof at the anchors. 45 feet

8. Whoa Nelly 5.11b ★

This climb is around left of *Wotai*, facing east. Up flakes and thin moves left of prow. 45 feet

9. Big Medicine 10b

Grey slab with thin moves, faces west. 55 feet

10. Pale Face Magic 10d

Climb up right facing corner then out right and up tricky, sharp face above. 55 feet

11. Medicine Man 11c ★★

Down around corner from *Pale Face Magic*, climb up dihedral, then out bulging wall to right. 50 feet

The following four routes are on the wall downhill and east of *Medicine Man*. 150 to 200 yards of bushwhacking will get you there. No photo.

12. The Ugly 11c

Face left of seam through small bulge. 40 feet

13. The Bad 11b

Clean face with thin pockets, moving left at top. 40 feet

14. The Good 11c

Prow/face to steeper rock above. 40 feet

15. Angel Eyes 5.11b

Climb prow between obvious cracks left of *The Good*. 4 bolts, sling anchor, 40 feet

WILD IRIS : Aspen Glades

A remuda is a herd of horses from which cowboys will choose their mounts for the day. The Remuda here is a small but shady crag where climbers can escape the sun on the hottest of summer days.

Routes are described right to left as they are encountered.

APPROACH (The Remuda)

The Remuda is best reached by heading north (downhill toward the Aspen Glade Wall) from the 4-way intersection at the dead trees. Keep right where the path splits, heading downhill into the trees keeping right of the drainage. Follow this trail for 10 to12 minutes (further than you think you should go...) until it reaches the beautiful clean walls that make up The Remuda. The trail reaches the wall near *Court n' Spark*.

---

17. Court n' Spark 12b ★★★

Good moves through thin face, then up nice prow. Ends on ledge. 55 feet

18. Buck a Move 13a

That's one small pocket! One short crux to much easier climbing above. 45 feet

19. The Devil's Herd 12a ★

Shares start with *Ghost Rider*, then moves right at upper bulge. 55 feet

20. Ghost Rider 11d ★

Up prow. Crux at bottom and at top. Popular but not classic. 55 feet

WILD IRIS : Aspen Glades

21. Pedophile Moustache 11c

Starts right of *Crooked Darlin'*, but climbs straight up, crossing
that route and ending slightly left. 5B 40 feet

22. Crooked Darlin' 11a

Diagonal line. A bit contrived, but easier than other route on the
wall. 7 bolts, 45 feet

**The following three routes are on the clean wall 100 feet
left of** *Crooked Darlin'*.

23. Burnt Beans and Coffee 12c ★★★

Long pulls between big pockets, with a tough crux at the end.
(no photo) 6 bolts, 60 feet

24. Silverbelly 12d ★★★

Up center of beautiful white wall, long moves on little pockets.
(no photo) 6 bolts, 55 feet

25. Coyote Vacuum 12b ★★

On the very left side of the *Silverbelly* wall, start in underclings,
then tricky moves to the top. (no photo) 5 bolts, 40 feet

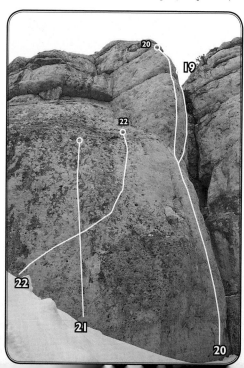

——— MINER'S DELIGHT ———

This wonderful wall is located southeast of Wyoming highway 28, across the road from the Wild Iris area. Climbing here has been going on since the early 1990s. Due to a long-ish approach and a scarcity of routes, it was left out of the last guidebook.

There are currently around twenty climbs on this south-facing wall, with room for many hundreds more. Conditions can be challenging; it's hot in the summers and impossible to access early season, short of hiking from the highway. Although the routes are few and far-between, some of the area's most singular pitches are on this wall. Many feel that *Rattlesnake Tambourine* is the best 12a in Lander.

> ## MINER'S DELIGHT ROUTE COUNT by GRADE
> ### 5.10 : 2 — 5.11 : 5 — 5.12 : 8 — 5.13 : 3

Brian Lenz pulling pockets on the classic *Arapahoe* (11d).
Photo © Bobby Model / M-11

GETTING THERE (Miner's Delight)

This cliff is reached by turning left (southeast) off Hwy 28 about 1/3 mile past Limestone Mountain Road (Wild Iris). This good dirt road curves around a slight hill, at which point you can see the crag in the distance. Follow the road down into a small meadow, keeping left at a small fork. As the road starts uphill, you'll head right on a less-traveled two-track (the main road goes left/north) which takes you to a clearing atop a small red cliffband. Park in this clearing and start hiking.

DRIVE TIME: 40 minutes from Lander

HIKE: 40 minutes uphill

SUN EXPOSURE: Sunny until 5 p.m. most of the year

SEASON: Summer and Fall

LENGTH: 40 to 90 feet

APPROACH (Miner's Delight)

Hike a contour to the east rather than straight up to the cliff – the climbs are about two miles east of the parking and the cliffband above the parking area does not have any routes on it. This trail is marked by cairns, and reaches the cliff near the singular arête pitch of *Arapahoe*.

MINER'S DELIGHT

1 & 2. Projects

3. Arapahoe 11d ★★★
Excellent arête, starts in left-facing corner/slot. 85 feet

4. Walk That Relish 12a ★
Slab to 45 degree headwall. 70 feet

5. Super Platinum Blonde 13a ★★
Steep wall with seam at start. 5 bolts, 50 feet

6. Red Right Hand 12b ★
Short wall with big moves. 45 feet

7. Abattoir Blues 13a/b ★★
Starts in a seam left of corner. Tricky. 45 feet

8. Tiger Sauce 11c ★
Slab to bulging wall. Hard-to-clip high anchor. 70 feet

9. White Trash Curry 11a
Slab with cracks to prow. Skip out-of-the-way last bolt. Sharp. 80 feet

10. The Undercling 11a ★★
Climbs finger crack/corner to roof, then traverses left under roof to vertical wall above. 60 feet

11. Johnny Lee's Corner 12c ★
Up same corner as previous route, then through sequential and strange roof encounter.

12. Anchovies 12a ★★
Vertical wall with a seam to a steeper wall. 10 bolts, 65 feet

13. King Lazybones 10b ★★
Layback flake to ledge. Short. Good warm-up. 40 feet

14. Project Leaning crack. Probably 5.10

15. Santa Cleopatra 11c
Tricky slab to a steeper wall. 70 feet

16. Totally Fully 13a ★
This climb takes a steep wall behind a large pine tree, about 150 yards right of the previous climb. 4 bolts, 40 feet

17. Yowzah 12a ★★★
Climbs a vertical wall with a seam to a cool, juggy 45 degree headwall. 75 feet

18. Rattlesnake Tambourine 12a ★★★
Climb a thin crack to a bulge, then up an awesome flake. Four stars. 50 feet

19. Last Year's Chili Queen 12c ★
Long pulls through low bulge, then up pockets. 60 feet

20. Ty's Route 12a no photograph
Right-leaning prow. 50 feet

21. The Leather Nun 10b no photograph
East-facing wall with neat pockets. Too short. 30 feet

MINER'S DELIGHT

SINKS CANYON

Sinks Canyon is the centerpiece of Lander climbing. Located just seven miles from downtown, this area features climbing on dozens of different cliffs consisting of three very different rock types. In a mere four miles, this unique canyon cuts through sandstone, dolomite and granite.

The original climbs in Sinks were on the cracks of the Sandstone cliffs near the canyon's mouth. As early as the 1950s, climbers were recording ascents of these intimidating walls. Major development of the sport climbing cliffs began years after climbers discovered the other walls of Sinks. It wasn't until the late 1980s, though, that the dolomite cliffs drew much attention. The period from about 1990 to 2000 saw massive development of the dolomite and, with over 320 climbable days a year, has seen a large influx of climbers from all over the world.

There are now over 550 routes in the canyon. The Sinks Canyon Road is open year round and in winter the Main Wall is the warmest and most sheltered from the wind. Summertime brings the heat, and most climbers escape to the higher crags of Fossil Hill and Wild Iris. For those seeking cool temps in the canyon this time of year, the Shady Side Crags are the best option.

Sinks Canyon Crags

Sandstone Crags : Begins on page 79

Bighorn Dolomite, The Shady Side : Begins on page 101

Bighorn Dolomite, Main Wall : Begins on page 108

Bighorn Dolomite, Fairfield Hill : Begins on page 152

Granite Crags : Begins on page 165

GETTING THERE (Sinks Canyon)

From Main Street in Lander, turn south on either 5th or 9th Street and go for less than a mile to where it T-bones with the "Sinks Canyon Road," Highway 131. Turn right. Just out of town, stay left where the Sinks Road forks with Squaw Creek Road. Continue almost 6 miles to the obvious entrance sign for the "Sinks Canyon State Park."

Sawmill Picnic Area is another 1/4 mile followed in the next mile and half or so by the State Park Visitor Center (limited hours) and then the Popo Agie Campground. All three of these facilities have restrooms and it is highly encouraged to use them before heading to the crags.

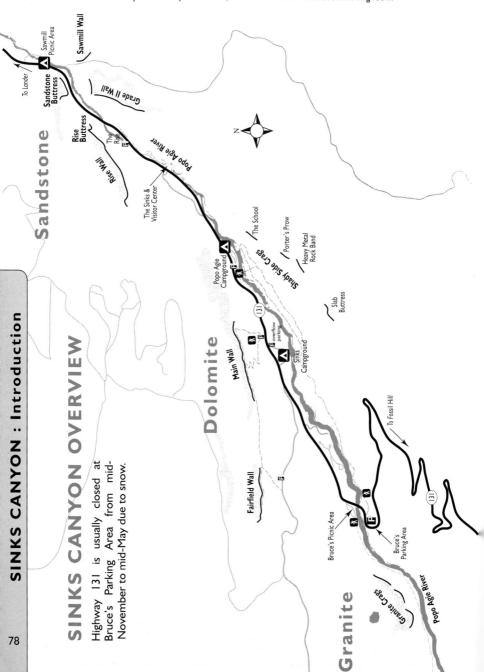

SINKS CANYON : Introduction

SINKS CANYON OVERVIEW

Highway 131 is usually closed at Bruce's Parking Area from mid-November to mid-May due to snow.

Sandstone

Dolomite

Granite

N

To Lander

Sawmill Picnic Area

Sawmill Wall

Sandstone Buttress

Grade II Wall

Rise Buttress

The Rise

Rise Wall

Popo Agie River

The Sinks & Visitor Center

The School

Porter's Prow

Heavy Metal Rock Band

Popo Agie Campground

Shady Side Crags

Slab Buttress

131

overflow parking

Sinks Campground

Main Wall

To Fossil Hill

Fairfield Wall

131

Bruce's Picnic Area

Bruce's Parking Area

Granite Crags

Popo Agie River

When driving into Sinks Canyon, the first beautiful walls you reach are the striped gray sandstone buttresses. These cliffs line the first few miles of the canyon and were the first cliffs that attracted climbers in the canyon. Recorded ascents date back to the 1950s, when climbers probably stopped off in the canyon for a few practice pitches on their way to the "real" climbing in the mountains above. In the 1960s and 70s, there was much activity in this area, as the sandstone was used as a primary training ground for the National Outdoor Leadership School.

These days, climbers visit the cliffs low in the canyon infrequently. Although a few classics such as *Gunky* and the *Standard Route* get almost weekly traffic, chances are you'll find yourself the only climbers at a given cliff, much as it was fifty years ago. Be aware that much of the hardware on these cliffs is dated and should be used with extreme caution. Fixed pins on any route were likely placed at least 25 years ago, and will likely not hold a fall.

Many of the climbs described here are going to be of nothing more than historical interest to many of us. But for climbers interested in an adventure and an appreciation for just how strong past climbers really were, the routes on these cliffs are worthy of a close look.

DRIVE TIME: 10 minutes from Lander

HIKE: 2 minutes uphill

SUN EXPOSURE: Sunny from 9a.m. to sunset

SEASON: Winter, Spring, Fall

LENGTH: 40 feet to several pitches

APPROACH (Sandstone Buttress)

Park at the large paved pullout on the right, just as you enter the canyon. The climbs on the left side of the wall are best accessed by hiking up the well-worn trail that leads uphill along the crag. For routes in the *Gunky* area, take the trail uphill to the point where the trail gets close to the wall, then approach the bases of the climbs via a wide ledge system. Below this wide ledge is the "Toprope Wall" which features several sets of fixed anchors on the ledge. Routes right of the Gunky area (starting at *Honeycomb*) can be accessed via a gully approach near the Toprope Wall, and then traversing right. The climbs near the Sentinel Cracks can be reached directly from the road below.

SANDSTONE ROUTE COUNT by GRADE

<5.7 : 12 — 5.8 : 12 — 5.9 : 7 — 5.10 : 31 — 5.11 : 18 — 5.12 : 13

Sandstone Buttress

This is the most popular of the sandstone walls. With an easy approach and descent, good parking, and warm, south-facing exposure, this is a great crag most of the year. There are several easier routes which are appropriate for teaching, as well as hard, scary testpieces. The canyon's most popular multi-pitch route, *Gunky*, sits as the centerpiece of this crag.

Above this buttress is a short band of limestone called the Boulder Band. This short wall holds dozens of well-traveled boulder problems and is a good place for a lonely climber to get a workout. The trail to this wall continues above the band to the west, eventually leading to a small "summit" recognized by a large dead tree near the top. This hike is a great training hill, providing 1,000 feet of vertical gain in a very short distance. This hike is a favorite of the legendary local Tom Hargis.

1. Unnamed Slab 10a ★

The leftmost climb on this wall, just right of a large juniper tree. Two bolts on a very featured face, then past a ledge and up lesser-quality climbing above. 4 bolts, 60 feet

2. The Longest Yard 10d

This climb starts above a small black cave, and the base is near a round granite boulder. Do an exposed traverse into a corner, then up. After about 20 feet, escape right on big holds. Above, move left and up slabby, easier moves to the top. Small cams, wires, 60 feet

3. New Sensations 12d ★

First of the new breed. Starts above a little black cave, moving up and right on big holds to a thin, hard crux. Clip a tatty thread, then continue up to a ledge. Above, move up and right to a hanging flake. Small cams or wires supplement quick draws.

4. The Maverick 12a ★

This route starts on a limestone band just right of two big junipers. Climb up to sandstone, through a small bulge, then follow bolts and drilled angles up a black streak right of some seams.

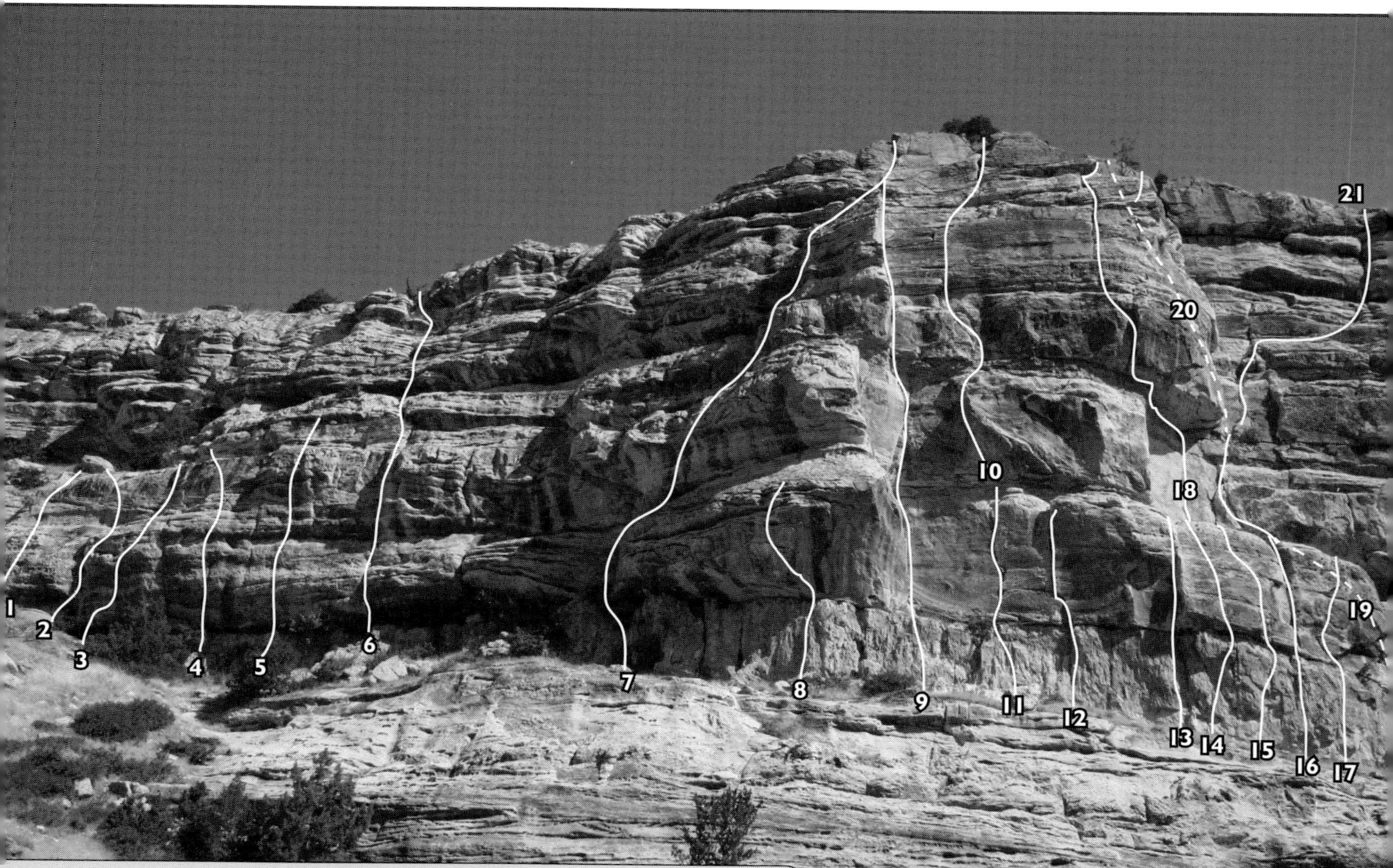
1
2
3
4
5
6
7
8
9
10
11
12
13
14
15
16
17
18
19
20
21

5. Dag Nab It 11a ★★

One of the first pure sport routes in Lander. Climb up the limestone wall and past the bushy horizontal then up a slabby wall to a right-facing overlap. 8 bolts, 70 feet

6. Friday the 13th 10d R

This climb starts in a right-facing corner capped by a square-cut white roof. Pass the roof, then follow rounded cracks that can be a bit bushy.

7. Barstool Grooves 5.6 R

Climb a widening crack up a left-facing corner to a ledge. Move right 15 feet on the ledge, then up a big, right-trending groove. Above, the route shares the final 20 feet with *Gunky*. Bring big gear and a broom.

8. Arapiles Revisited 12b ★

A classic of sorts, used to be the "must do" route for the grade. Less popular since the swell of so many great 12b routes in the area. Crank up face, then out the big bulge on sloping, big holds. The wall above is yet to be climbed.

9. Gunky 8 ★★★

A pretty climb, this is a two or three-pitch affair with a wide variety of climbing. Fixed anchors. Standard rack.

10. Funky Monkey 11c

This climb takes the steep, leaning seam above *No Name Crack*. After the initial intimidating crux moves, the climbing eases off above. 90 feet

11. No Name Crack 7 ★★

This is the first crack right of *Gunky*, a left-facing flake to a bolted anchor at a ledge. Gear to 3 inches. 40 feet

12. Standard Start 5 ★

Another left-facing crack that gets good and wide near the top. Anchors at ledge. 40 feet

13. Cardboard Crack 8

This is a left-facing dihedral with a nice brown patina that leads to a funky overlap. Climb up to ledge on easier moves. 45 feet

SINKS CANYON : Sandstone

14. Ryan's Romp 11a ★

This sport route climbs up steep limestone to a sandstone slab above with a seam. Really fun climbing on this and the following three climbs. 50 feet

15. Zen the Cat 10c ★★

Up a highly bolted limestone wall to the slab above. 50 feet

16. Brady's Sandbox 10a

Follow a bolted limestone wall to a crack above. Small rack up to 2.5 inches. 50 feet

17. Lucky's Refuge 11b ★★

Again, limestone climbing leads to technical sandstone slab climbing above, up a right-facing feature. 50 feet

18. Jump For Juniper 11b R

A standard-setting route at the time of the first ascent. Climb the first pitch of the *Standard Route*. At the ledge, step left to a 5.9 corner crack below a roof. Climb up to a band of broken rock, then traverse left under the roof. Turn the roof at an odd slot feature, then negotiate some scary, thin moves. Continue up on less-steep and easier ground. Two pitches. Standard rack.

19. Standard Route 5 ★

This route starts in the major gully right of *Gunky*. Pitch one climbs up easy stone to nice ledges. Above, stay right of the corner/roof by climbing cracks on the face. Use cracks and corners to reach a short chimney and then exit onto a big ledge. The third pitch follows a much easier corner for about 40 feet to the top. Standard rack.

20. Dare 8 R

A variation to the last pitch of the *Standard Route*. From near the top of the chimney, step right and up a nice, but scary, slab. Small cams, wire. 40 feet

21. Armadillo Exit 9 R

Follows the first pitch and half of the second on *Standard Route*. Move right at a small stance to a left-facing, rounded crack. Can be done in either two or three pitches.

22. D.O.A. 9 R

This is the corner just right of the *Standard Route*. Pitch one follows a corner to a ledge, then up and left on liebacks. Climb face holds to a ledge and belay. Pitch two can be done by moving left to join the *Armadillo Exit*, or by traversing right and finishing up the final pitch of *Honeycomb*. Standard rack with extra small cams.

23. Honeycomb 10a R ★

Pitch one follows a corner, traverses left, then up easy terrain to a belay at a ledge. The fun pitch two climbs steep huecos, hen traverses slightly right to a crack ending at a large stance and a belay. The third pitch takes easy stone to a 5.8 exit crack. Bring a small rack and some extra medium and long slings.

24. Haldicheck 8 ★

Pitch one takes a sandy corner through an overhang, ending on a spacious ledge. Above, climb the right-facing corner, ending on a ledge at a bolted belay. Continue to the top via a large, flaring crack. Standard rack.

25. Group Grope 10c R ★

This intimidating route takes steep corners and flakes left of the *Sentinel Chimney*. First done in three pitches, it's possible to link pitches one and two. Lots of small pro.

Toprope Wall

This short wall sits below the Sandstone Buttress route *Honeycomb*. These climbs feature fixed anchors along the top of the cliff, which is the wide ledge below the main buttress. Approach from the left as coming up directly from the road is really unpleasant bushwhacking. *Code Blue* and *Road Test* are both worthwhile climbs. Climbs are best found by locating the anchors on the ledge above. The routes are listed left-to-right. No Photo.

A. Unnamed 7

B. Unnamed 8

C. Lateral 10

D. Dorsal 10

E. Code Blue 11

F. Road Test 12a

SINKS CANYON : Sandstone

21

23

24

22

Top Rope Wall

26. Sentinel Chimney 7 ★★

This semi-classic climbs up a squeeze to a ledge, then up a corner to a second ledge and a belay. Above, climb the chimney to another ledge and belay, or continue a bit higher to link itches 2 and 3. Above, climb ramp/cracks to top. Rap the route or walk off right. Small rack and several slings.

27. Sentinel Cracks 8 ★

This route takes left-facing corners right of the chimney. One pitch or two short ones get you to a big ledge. Traverse left to join *Sentinel Chimney* or rappel. Standard rack.

28. Sentinel Crack Direct 11a R

A face route with three bolts.

29. Sandy But Dandy Direct 10a R

Hard-to-protect corner and crack that leads to the end of the opening traverse of *Sandy But Dandy*. After joining that route for a pitch, head straight up over a small roof. After you surmount the overhang (crux), finish on easier ground.

30. Sandy But Dandy 8 ★

Start by traversing along a prominent, left-leaning lieback crack. At the end of the crack, head straight up another crack system in a left-facing corner, finishing at a small pod stance below an overhang. Move 20-30 feet right into a prominent right-facing corner to finish. Standard rack.

31. Five Year Plan 12a

Face/slab with cool movement. Clip four drilled angles, supplementing with thin gear, and belay at a welcome ledge. Finishes on *Sandy But Dandy*.

32. Baby d'Angles 11d

A slightly easier climb than *Five Year Plan*, protects with small gear and drilled angles.

33. Gravity in Chains 10d

The easiest and best of the bolted slabs on the right side of the buttress, this one ends at a nice ledge.

34. Illusions of Lander 11b X

Slab with thin gear and notoriously bad bolts. Best not to fall.

35. Rick's Roof 8

This climb is located in the alcove above the previous routes.

SINKS CANYON : Sandstone

87

Rise Buttress

This is the next wall up canyon from the Sandstone Buttress. It features an orange-colored prow above the bridge where the road crosses the Popo Agie River just below the Rise. To reach the crag, park near the bridge and follow game trails up to the base. Climbs are described right-to-left, as one approaches.

1. The Howl 10d ★

This climb is the first crack on the right side of the buttress. Follow a varying crack in a corner system. Cruise through awkward moves, then up through a rough roof move. Easier climbing leads through a second roof near the top. Standard rack

2. Asleep at the Wheel 7

Not popular, this is the next crack left of *The Howl*. Follow a nice crack to a slanting ledge, then fight up wide junk to the top. Bring goggles.

3. Fear of Flying 10d R

Junky rock leads to a fun (?) hand-to-fist crack, to more junk.

4. D.O.E. 12b ★

Fun, rail riding sport route. Through a cool rail roof and up sandy face above. 50 feet

5. ScAiry 11c

One of the more singular pitches in the canyon. Follow a thin crack to a rightward traverse along a horizontal/ledge. Step out onto the rounded prow and enjoy the air below. Bring long slings.

6. Adelita 10c ★★

Start same as *ScAiry*, but move left at the end of the initial crack. Finish on *Green Wall*.

7. Green Wall 8

This is the major crack system. Looks nice, not so nice.

8. Wee Doggies 12a ★

This is a great, leaning crack in a corner. The best of the sandstone 5.12s.

Rise Wall

The Rise Wall is the massive and intimidating wall that sits above the Rise of the Popo Agie. You can reach the wall by parking at the Rise, and following faint trails uphill. These climbs aren't as popular as they used to be, so established trails are nonexistent. Climbs are described right-to-left, as one approaches.

9. Way Roof 10b

Scramble up 4th and 5th class terrain to a stance below a high and prominent roof. This is a right-facing roof crack climb.

10. If It's Tuesday in Wyoming 10a

This climb takes a clean left-facing corner into an adventurous groove.

11. Made For Aid 12a TR

This thin crack climbs the center of the varnished wall. Originally aided, then toproped free. May still be awaiting a free lead.

SINKS CANYON : Sandstone

12. The Buzz 10d R

The big brother of *The Sting*. Climb up to an obvious hanging
spike, then up the thin left side of the orange pillar. Join *The Sting*
for one pitch. From the ledge atop pitch 2, climb straight up and
through the stout offwidth roof.

13. The Sting 10a ★★

The best route on this section of wall. Climb discontinuous
corners to reach the left side of the obvious orange pillar, and
then climb it to its top. Move into the chimney, then left out
its top (crux) and climb to the big ledge above. Exit the wall by
scrambling right.

14. Dumb Bunnies 9

This climb takes a roof crack/groove/grovel on the right side of
a prominent white roof. Not that great.

15. Fat Back 10b

This route is on the short wall below the ramp up to *The Snake*.
Climb a non-cool groove to a handcrack through a left-facing
roof crack.

16. The Snake 8

To reach this route hike up grass ramps and ledges 50-70 yards left of *The Sting*. Scramble up a low-angle slab into a prominent left-facing corner (5.7) and climb it to a ledge. Traverse left on this ledge about 60 feet and then take another corner to the top.

17. Freak Factor 9

This climb starts just right of *The Dungeon*. Take a clean offwidth crack that parallels *The Dungeon* and joins it at the belay.

Share pitch two's chimney with *The Dungeon*. Move right at the chockstone for a character-building ramble to the top of the wall.

18. The Dungeon 8

This climb takes the big corner system in the middle of the Rise Wall. It starts just left of a prominent overhanging prow. Follow left-facing flakes in a grey-white corner to a bolted belay at a ledge below the chimney.

Pitch two climbs this big chimney to a belay at a stance below a big-ass chockstone. Move left and up a thin crack above.

SINKS CANYON : Sandstone

19. Leaning Pillar 7

This small pillar has two climbs on either side of it, both 5.7.
This is about halfway between *Hawk Walk* and *The Dungeon*. Rap
from the top. No photo. 60 feet

20. Eagle Dance 11a

This is a variation to the start of *The Eagle*. This is a left-leaning
layback with some fixed gear.

21. The Eagle 10c ★

Climb up limestone for about 10 feet, then make hard moves to
a right-leaning crack. Take this into the left-leaning crack above.
Once established in this crack, the climbing eases up. Climb to a
ledge, then up easier rock to a second ledge. Follow the easy (5.7)
crack above to the top of the wall. Standard rack

22. Hawk Walk 10d ★★

Pitch one takes a cool left-facing flake to a nice ledge (5.7). Above,
work left and up through overhanging terrain to an easier crack
above. The crux can be avoided by joining pitch 2 of *The Eagle*.

Franklin's Tower

Higher in the canyon, to the left of the Rise Wall, is Franklin's Tower. This blond-colored open book is a nice looking chunk of rock. For climbs on Franklin's Tower and Hawk Walk, it might be best to approach from the Visitor Center parking area, as it gives you a slightly higher starting elevation. No photograph.

23. Franklin's Tower 10b R

This is the big, light-colored corner. Climb wide cracks and ledges (5.10) to a belay stance. Above, the climbing is in a thinner and easier crack.

24. Zombie Dance 7 ★

This climb takes varied corners and ledges left of the main corner.

Sawmill Wall

The Sawmill Wall boasts a high concentration of hard routes, and the best sandstone in the canyon. In the late 1980s, this crag was the scene of all the hard climbing action in the area. With the rise in popularity of climbing on the steeper, more solid dolomite stone, this wall has fallen out of popularity.

APPROACH (The Sawmill)

Sawmill is the first cliff you pass on the way into Sinks Canyon. It's located on the left side of the road, across the Popo Agie river, just upstream from the last house (a geodesic dome). Do not approach this wall via the driveway to this house. Rather, park at the Sawmill picnic ground or the Sandstone Buttress parking area, and cross the river. Once on the other side, you'll walk downstream, cross the shallow Sawmill Creek, and reach this west-facing wall.

---

1. Born To Be A Cowboy 12b ★

This climb is a thin left-facing corner that starts right where the electric fence is bolted to the cliff (this will make sense when you see it). Tech stem and tips liebacking. Be suspicious of the 20+ year-old pin placements! Zero-type cams are useful.

2. Open Project

This climbs a cool clean face to a smooth groove. Looks wild!

3. Good, Bad, and Ugly 10c ★

Follow the thin seams and edges right of the big dihedral. Small cams and nuts supplement bolts.

4. Main Street Cattle Drive 12a ★★

A classic of sorts, this climb takes the line of edges and seams just right of the center of the clean face.

5. High Noon 11c ★★

Follow good edges and cracks just left of the prow/arête. Drilled angles for pro should be scrutinized.

6. Ghetto Blaster 11a

A left-facing corner capped by a high roof. Gets wide at the lip.

7. Project The Defender

This takes a steep crack to a thin roof encounter, then climbs into soft rock above. Should be good when it gets clean.

8. Blasted Cactus 10c

A cool feature that's prettier to look at than to climb. Start in the left crack of a box chimney. The crack gets thinner/more pleasant as you climb higher.

9. Dead Bird Crack 9

A nice hand crack turns ugly as you get higher.

10. Gold-Plated Wall

These climbs are all on the beautiful wall right of *Dead Bird Crack*. This is arguably the best sandstone in Sinks. Bolted anchors protect these routes. Access them by scrambling up from the right. Climbs listed left-to-right.

A. Gold Plated #1 12a TR

B. Gold Plated #2 12b TR

C. Gold Plated #3 11d TR

D. Gold Plated #4 11b TR

E. Gold Plated #5 11c TR

F. Gold Plated #6 9 TR

SINKS CANYON : Sandstone

SINKS CANYON : Sandstone

95

Grade II Wall

The Grade II Wall faces north and sits directly across the canyon from the Rise Wall. For routes 1-4, one can scramble up left of the cliff to gain the belay ledge between pitches one and two, identified by a band of limestone that splits the cliff.

APPROACH (Grade II Wall)

This wall is best accessed by parking at The Rise Parking Area, crossing the road, and then crossing the dry riverbed. Work uphill on game trails to the base of the wall. For routes on the left end of the cliff, cutting a contour across the hill makes for a really easy approach. Note that for most of the month of June, the otherwise dry riverbed is a raging torrent, when spring runoff overflows the cave where the river sinks underground.

Limestone Band

SINKS CANYON : Sandstone

1. Waiting For George, Left 10b

Climb either a nasty 5.7 slot or scramble up a left-leaning gully to gain the limestone band ledge. Move right and then up to a good, right-leaning corner. Take this past ledges, and up a nice section of stone, finishing on a good ledge. Rap off or continue to the top on sketchy 5.9 terrain.

2. Waiting For George, Right 5

This climb takes the same start as *Waiting For George, Left.* From the limestone band, follow the same initial corner as the previous route, but go right where the crack splits at ledges. Above, move back left and finish up blocky terrain (5.9) or rap off.

3. Amanitas 9 ★★

Start as for *Waiting for George* or traverse in along the ledge. This is a left-facing corner to a roof to a great crack. From the second ledge, you can climb a scary 5.9 pitch straight above or traverse left or right to adjacent routes. Most climbers do only pitch two of this route.

4. Belladonna 10a ★★

Climb any number of crack/face options to reach the limestone band, or traverse in from the left. Lieback up a right-facing corner (9-) to the second ledge and a bolted belay. The third pitch moves right and then attacks the cool roof above, the route's crux. Standard Rack and small cams.

5. Ego Tripper 6

This is the major corner system left of a big blank section of wall. Start about 50 feet left of the obvious right-facing flake corner at the base. A short face climbing section with a bolt leads to an easy crack, which takes you to the ledge. Climb through the limestone band just right of two large bushes, and up a right-facing corner. Belay at a block-covered ledge. Easier climbing up cracks and ledges leads to the summit.

6. Genius of Horror 11c X

A crazy man's route. Just right of a big right-facing flake/corner, this is a slab to a skinnier right-facing corner. The corner becomes a roof near its top. Follow the roof right and escape onto the ledge above. Small cams make this more protectable than it was during the first ascent, but it's still very serious.

7. Fear and Loathing 12a ★

Pitch one of this climb starts up low-angled rock, and is protected by a couple of old bolts. From the ledge at the limestone band, climb up into a right-facing flake. Follow this up and through a small overhang to a nice belay below a rounded crack. Climb this crack, that goes from easy to very hard in a hurry. After the steep finger/hand section that makes up the crux of the climb, plan on a short section of wide crack to earn the top of the wall.

8. Avalanche 11b R

This serious outing starts with a 5.8 slab just right of a hanging flake. Belay at the limestone band. Above, thin crack climbing with challenging pro takes you up a right-facing corner, past a small ledge and to a belay at an alcove. Above, the line steepens, and the crack becomes a hard-to-protect flare. Follow this to a ledge/slab with a tree. From here, move right along a low angle crack to exit the wall.

9. Unemployment Line 10c

Climb up a low-angle slab to a ledge with a small bush below the limestone band. Follow bolts through the band to a right-facing corner/flake system. After about 60 feet, the corner leans right and eventually hits a small roof. Before reaching the roof, move left on face moves to rounded ledges. Continue to traverse left to a right-facing corner which you can take to the top.

Limestone Band

SINKS CANYON : Sandstone

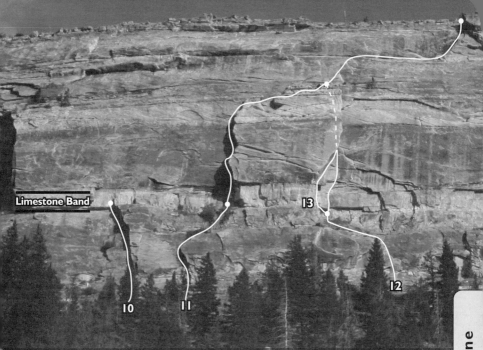

Limestone Band

10

11

13

12

10. Four Dead Aliens 10d ★

This route takes a left facing corner about 30 feet left of *Mitten*. Climb up on thin cam placements, widening as you go. A right exit near the belay is the more pleasant finish. 70 feet

11. Mitten, Left Side 10b ★★

Pitch one takes a left-facing overlap that tends to be damp early season and tends to be wide and difficult year-round. Belay at the limestone band at the base of the *Mitten* flake. More awkward, yet clean, climbing takes you to the top of the flake. Traverse right to belay. Above, climb a short bolted slab, then move right on ledges to an easy left-facing corner.

12. Mitten, Right Side 8 R

Pitch one is an easy approach ramp from the right. Above, climb up crack to gain the chimney, a sporty, sandy affair. At the top of the flake, the route continues up a slab on bolts, then right and up an easy corner.

13. The Boxer 10b ★

This is a fun variation to *Mitten, Right Side*. Climb a steep crack in a right-leaning corner to join *Mitten* halfway up its second pitch.

14. Hooter's Holiday 10a R

This climb is at the far right end of the Grade II Wall. Standard rack with extra micro cams. Start in right-facing cracks, moving left at the limestone band and up a right-facing feature to a big ledge (5.8) The serious second pitch takes a thin crack up to a difficult face move, steps right, and up a right-facing dihedral.

15. Royal Edge 7 ★★

This three pitch route doesn't get the attention it deserves. Standard Rack. Start up right-facing cracks, belaying at a large ledge after about 80 feet. The second pitch takes the corner system above, passing several nice stances. Pitch three moves left and up to the top on liebacks and good jams. One can also move right into the next corner to finish the climb. This alternate third pitch is also 5.7.

Limestone Band

14

15

SINKS CANYON : Shady Side

The sunny walls of Sinks Canyon's Main Wall and Fairfield Hill are what bring climbers to the canyon, but that's not all the dolomite there is. On the tree-covered north-facing side of the canyon, long expanses of this great stone peek above the soon-to-be-dead forest providing climbers with a nice respite from the heat in summer months.

Starting across the river from the Sinks Canyon State Park Visitor Center, there are four major dolomite outcrops. From left to right, they are The School, Porter's Prow, The Heavy Metal Rock Band, and the Slab Buttress. The first three of these are described below. The Slab Buttress has only one existing route and will not be covered in this guide.

DRIVE TIME: 12 minutes from Lander

HIKE: 15-20 minutes uphill

SUN EXPOSURE: Shady until 2 or 3 p.m., some partial shade

SEASON: Late Spring, Summer, Early Fall

LENGTH: 40 to 120 feet

SHADY SIDE PITCH COUNT by GRADE
<5.7 : 3 — 5.8 : 3 — 5.9 : 2 — 5.10 : 5 — 5.11 : 15 — 5.12 : 5

The School

Also known as the "Cool Crag" this wall was first explored by Kirk Billings in the mid 1990s. It has since seen much development, with a huge impact on the area below the crag. This is mostly thanks to large groups led by educational organizations (ironically) teaching Leave No Trace ethics. There are many great moderates here that can be enjoyed all summer long. Routes listed from right to left.

APPROACH (The School)

Park at the Popo Agie Campground, and hike across the swinging bridge over the Popo Agie River. On the far side of the bridge, the trail splits. You'll want to go straight ahead and up some short steps on a trail heading toward the cliffs on the hill above. After about 3-4 minutes on this trail, it forks. Go left, hiking another 3-4 minutes to another fork. Take the right fork at a sign that indicates you're headed for "climbing." Follow this trail uphill to the cliff.

1. Cool Whip 11a ★ no picture

This climb is approached by walking left and downhill from where the trail meets the wall. After about 50 yards, you go uphill again, and then walk back right along a large ledge. Both this route and Ice Cream take nice lines above this ledge. 40 feet

2. Ice Cream 11d ★ no picture

Just right of *Ice Cream*. Nice rock. 40 feet

3. Sorting Hat Left 10a

This is the leftmost route on the low-angle wall where the trail reaches the cliff. Starts near a tree, climbing on big holds to a thinner finish. 10 bolts, 55 feet

4. Sorting Hat Right 7 ★

This climb takes the middle line up the slab, reaching the same anchors as *Sorting Hat Left*. 10 bolts, 55 feet

5. C'est Fini 9 ★

The right line on the slab. 10 bolts, 60 feet

6. Finish Your Homework 9/11a ★★

This climb and *The Grand Adventure* have been erroneously referred to as *Ice Cream* and *Cool Whip* for years. This climb is on the wall right of where the trail meets the wall. There is a big, dirty corner right of *C'est Fini*. This climb is about 15 feet right of that. The bottom wall is mostly jugs, with an anchor at a small ledge about 40 feet up (5.9). Above, the route works left and up on more difficult rock.

7. The Grand Adventure 8/11a/11c ★★

This route has almost as many anchors as protection bolts. The first "pitch" is an excellent moderate at 5.8. Above, the route climbs a difficult slab to another set of anchors (11a). Continuing through the roof above leads to the route's crux (11c) and a third set of anchors.

8. Banish Misfortune 6/10a ★

Uphill and right of the previous route, this climb takes a crack system (5.6) to a mid-way anchor, then on up a steeper wall. 12 bolts, 60 feet

9. Imaginary Fans 8/10c ★★

Fifteen feet right of *Banish Misfortune*. Up an easier wall to a bulge (and sub-anchor) and crux above. 12 bolts, 60 feet

10. K-School 8

A variation to *Imaginary Fans*, this route jogs right from the first set of anchors on that route. 60 feet

Porter's Prow

This is a series of nice-looking gold corners above the Sinks Canyon nature trails. This small crag has just five routes, but is a nice respite from the summer's heat.

APPROACH (Porter's Prow & Heavy Metal Rock Band)

Park at the Popo Agie Campground, and hike across the swinging bridge over the Popo Agie River. On the far side of the bridge, the trail splits. You'll want to go straight ahead and up some short steps on a trail heading toward the cliffs on the hill above.

After about 3-4 minutes on this trail, it forks. Go right, following the path until you hit a buck-and-rail fence. Just after crossing the fence, turn left and follow faint game trails alongside the fence line up into the woods. Eventually, these solidify into a major trail heading up the drainage between Porter's Prow and the Heavy Metal Rock Band.

As the angle steepens and the gully narrows. A faint climbers' trail breaks left and over to Porter's. The crag is visible at this junction and should be easy to find. The Porter climbs are listed from left to right.

The HMRB is to the right of this gully. About 2 minutes uphill from Porter's, a climbers' trail breaks left along the base of this crag. Routes 1-4 area very near the left end of the crag, while route 12-15 are at the very-right end, about 5 minutes' walk away.

---

1. The Jazz Singer 11c

Left of the major prow, this climb takes low-angle rock up a black streaked wall just right of a corner system with several prominent flakes. 85 feet

2. Porter's Prow Left 11d ★

This route has tan pained hangers and starts six feet right of *Jazz Singer*. Follow a line just right of the main prow to anchors visible on the skyline. 75 feet

3. Porter's Prow 11c ★★

This is the central prow line. 70 feet

4. Porter's Steep Side 11c ★★

This climb takes steep stone just right of the main prow.

5. Dancing With Godzilla 11b

This is the rightmost route on the cliff. It takes the cleanest section of the not-so-clean face right of the main prow.

Heavy Metal Rock Band

1. Go Dog Go! 11b ★ no photo

This route about 50 yards from the left end of the cliffband. The first part of this route follows a left-leaning seam, then tackles good climbing above. The seam catches some run-off so can be a bit dirty. 70 feet

2. Goodnight Gorilla 12b ★★

Climb up nice moves to a low roof, then right and up to a vertical wall with hard-to-see pockets. 5 bolts, 50 feet

3. Animal Sounds 12b ★

Similar to *Goodnight Gorilla*, but without the roof. Feels more tenuous than it is. 7 bolts, 55 feet

4. Goodnight Moon 12d ★★

A crazy and cool set of moves. Starts in small corner under a high roof, then moves left to a prow and up to end near the left edge of the roof. 5 bolts, 40 feet

5. Spinal Tap 11c ★★

This is the left most line on the tall, clean central wall. 70 feet

6. The Amp That Goes to 11! 12a

The next route left, up thin pockets on a ever-steepening wall. Still dirty. 70 feet

7. When The Levee Breaks 12b ★★

The right route on the wall, best identified by the large hueco at bolt two. 75 feet

SINKS CANYON : Shady Side

8. Dennis and Jacques' Excellent Adventure 11a ★★

This is a fun route that climbs up a short wall, then over a small overlap to a steeper headwall. 7 bolts, 60 feet

9. Variation to D and J 11a

This route is close to, and shares holds with *Dennis and Jacques*. The upper wall was bolted at the time of the FA, and this variation now makes an independent line.

10. Stairway to Heaven 11a

This is a long prow route, which makes an interesting ramble.

11. Paula's Arête 6 ★ no photo

One of the better dolomite moderates, this climb is slightly hidden partway up a large gully, about 50 yards right of *Stairway to Heaven*.

12. Project Styff Kittens

Steep wall just left of the very prominent arête. 50 feet

13. Project

Leftmost line on the pretty golden wall. 50 feet

14. George's Last Stand 10d ★

This is a pretty nice climb. Heads up the center of the gold wall to anchors below crappy rock. 65 feet.

15. Indian Summer 10c

This climb is the right most route on the yellow-orange wall at the right end of the cliff. A small square-cut roof identifies the start of this climb. 7 bolts, 60 feet.

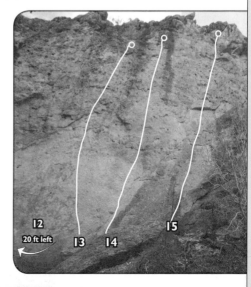

SINKS CANYON : Main Wall

SINKS CANYON : Main Wall

The Main Wall of Sinks is, arguably, the most consistently climbable crag in the country; this wall is good both in mid-winter and mid-summer. As the sun rises higher in the sky during the summer months, the crag tends to get more shade, in the arctic cold of the Wyoming winter, an inversion and great sun exposure keep the wall toasty hot on sunny days.

The Main Wall saw little attention until the early 1990s, when Greg Collins and a small group of other climbers realized the potential that lay before them. Over the ensuing years the route count has grown to over 260, including 52 routes 5.13 and harder. The huge variety of grades, the many different angles, and the consistently good weather make this a prime choice for any season.

DRIVE TIME: 12 minutes from Lander

HIKE: 10 to 15 minutes uphill

SUN EXPOSURE: Sunny until 3 p.m. most of the year

SEASON: Winter, Spring, Fall, and Summer evenings

LENGTH: 40 to 110 feet

MAIN WALL ROUTE COUNT by GRADE

< 5.9 : 22	—	5.10 : 44	—	5.11 : 70
5.12 : 74	—	5.13 : 45	—	5.14 : 7

The routes are listed right to left across the entire cliff (numbers 1 to 253), and grouped loosely into sub areas (usually named for that section's best known route).

To help you orient yourself, these sub-areas are marked on the wide-angle panorama across the following pages.

Photo opposite: Mattie Sheafor on the
three star classic, *Bush Doctor* (12a).
Photo © Steve Bechtel.

PANORAMA ABOVE : SINKS CANYON : Main Wall

A. Scud Wall & Pinnacle; **B.** Killer Cave : Right; **C.** Killer Cave : Left;
D. Harvest Moon Wall; **E.** Camel Jockey Wall; **F.** Happy Wheel Wall;
G. The Brisket Wall; **H.** White Heat Wall; **I.** Addiction Wall;
J. Citadel Wall; **K.** Hardware Wall; **L.** Face Dancer Wall; **M.** Moss Cave;
N. Purple Galaxy Wall; **O.** Achin' for Bootie Wall & The Wilds;
P. Squaretop Boulder; **Q.** Wave Mutilation Boulder; **R.** Fairfield Hill.

APPROACH (Main Wall)

The Main Wall is located 2.6 miles from the entrance to the canyon, with the primary parking being on the right side of the road, approximately 100 yards past the cattle guard. Additional parking is available down canyon 1/4 mile on the south side. The trail leaves the primary parking lot from the right corner, and splits after just a few feet at the trailhead sign.

When the parking lot is full PLEASE use the overflow area rather than parking along the road.

Routes 1 to 117 : Follow the right-hand trail, (Killer Cave Trail).
Routes 118 to 253 : Follow the left-hand trail (Addiction Trail).
Routes 254 to 268 : On large boulders below the main cliffs.

The Squaretop Boulder is best reached via parking at the Fairfield Hill road (0.4 miles past the main parking area).
The Wave of Mutilation Boulder can be reached by walking the Addiction Trail to the first switchback, then angling downhill toward the road and around to the south face of the boulder.

Mike Anderson on *Endeavor* (13c).
Photo © Steve Bechtel

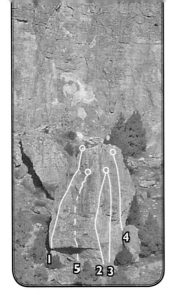

Scud Pinnacle ──────────

1. West Ridge 5 (requires gear)
Climb 50 foot prow to web anchors.

2. Spank the Monkey 11d ★
A decent climb up the south side arête. 50 feet

3. Monkeys on the Moon 11c
Take the center of the steep southeast side. 45 feet

4. Monkey Man 10c ★
Climb up off block along seams to a high anchor. 45 feet

5. Monkey Wrench 9
On the back side of the Scud Pinnacle.

Scud Wall ──────────────────

6. Scud Alert 10a
Good pockets up short wall. Left and right variations have been equipped with 2-3 bolts each. Both are silly. 40 feet

7. Storm of the Century 10d ★★
Hard start leads to very good headwall climbing. 55 feet

8. Rubber Soul 11a ★
Easy climbing to tricky bulge. 55 feet

9. Girl's Day Out 6
Face climbing and ledge mantling. 60 feet

10. Mei Day 6
Up corner and low angle face. 60 feet

11. You Go, Girl 10d
Start in corner, then move out onto prow to join *Boy, I Gotta Go*. A bit contrived. 45 feet

12. Boy, I Gotta Go 10a ★★
A very popular prow route. 45 feet

13. Atta Boy, Girl 9 ★

Up pockets and seam to leftward traverse that ends sharing the *Climb Like a Girl* anchors. 50 feet

14. Climb Like a Girl 10a ★

Thin crimps and longer moves, then through small roof above. 50 feet

15. Stud Alert 10c ★★

Move through low overhang to easier slab, then through a 3-foot roof at the top. 50 feet

16. Duck Soup 9 ★★★

Climb up flakes to a steeper wall above. 50 feet

17. Banoffee 10a ★★

Continuous slabby face. 50 feet

18. Doggin' Dude 8 ★

Climb up seam feature to slab above. 50 feet

Killer Cave : Right

19. Action Candy 10a ★★
Long route with many bolts, continuous moderate moves. 80 feet

20. King of Hearts 10d ★
Hard moves low to easy climbing, then through tricky bulge and up slab above. 80 feet

21. Back-up Binkie 12a
Hard bouldery start to easy slab, then up to anchors. 60 feet

22. Second-Hand Nova 11a ★★
Start on thin crimps, moving up and left to a seam. Up face above to small roof. 55 feet

23. Spook Eyes 12b
Start on the right end of big bulge, just behind the big tree. Very powerful start leads to fun, easier climbing to the top. 60 feet

24. Comin' Home Curly 14a ★
Starts as *One Love*, but break right at bolt three. Hard monos. See photo on Dedication Page. 65 feet

25. One Love 13c ★★
Hard pulls through low bulge, then up vertical wall to another hard roof at the top. 65 feet

26. Endeavor to Stab Bush 13c
This hybrid links the *Endeavor* start to the cruxes of *Clown Stabber* and *Bush Doctor*. 75 feet

27. Endeavor to Persevere 13c ★★★
Climb up center of belly, starting on the big boulder. The hard bit is getting to the undercling crack, then it's just some enduro 13a climbing to the anchors. 75 feet

SINKS CANYON : Main Wall

114

Neil Humphrey climbing *Action Candy* (10a).
Photo © Ken Driese. January 1997.

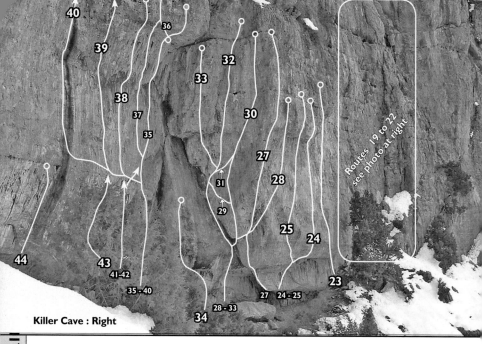

Killer Cave : Right

28. Jimmy Wings Not Included 12c ★

Again, the same start as *Bush Doctor*. After bolt three, traverse right along the undercling, crossing *Endeavor* and turning to the right side of the prow. Up face and through small roof. Not as contrived as it sounds, and pretty fun. 70 feet

29. Dr. Endeavor 13a ★★

This popular hybrid starts on *Bush Doctor*, then traverses on *Endeavor* at bolt number three. 75 feet

30. Clown Stabber 12d ★

Same start as *Bush Doctor*, then right into bulge after bolt three. Long moves to easy corner above. 75 feet

31. Bloodline 11d ★★

Same as *Bush Doctor*, but traverses right to a big dihedral after bolt six (This route actually is a combo of *Bush Doctor* and *Clown Stabber*). 75 feet

32. Bush Doctor 12a ★★★

Start in a major corner above a big boulder. If the start is done from the ground (*sans* cheater blocks/log) this route is 12b. Climb up corner, through bulge, then straight up after bolt six. 75 feet

Killer Cave : Right

33. Ring of Fire 12c ★

Shares the *Bush Doctor* start, but moves left after bolt six, through the small roof and up a steep prow. 75 feet

34. The Urchin 13a ★★

Short and powerful route, starts in undercling/lieback corner, up and over bulge. 45 feet

35. Zero Degrees 13c ★

Climbs up *Baghdad's* corner, then straight up to an anchor (12a). Go out the big roof above. 75 feet

36. Cannonball 12c ★

Splits left from *Zero Degrees* at the anchor below the roof and diagonals past 4 bolts on juggy holds. 75 feet

37. Deadman's Reach 12c ★

Follows *Zero Degrees* to just past the rest flake at half-height, then splits left and continues up through roof. Shares lip encounter with *Cannonball*. 75 feet

38. Baghdad 12c ★

Climb left-facing corner to horizontal, traverse left and up big holds through steep wall above. 75 feet

117

39. Basra 12c

Start as for *Baghdad*, but continue left along horizontal to next line of bolts. Climb up and through steeps above. 80 feet

40. House of God 13a

Start in *Baghdad's* left-facing corner, up to horizontal pocket band, then left all the way to black streak and up. 100 feet

41. Shao Lin Shadow Boxing 13b

Hard pulls between positive holds. Join *Baghdad* to finish. 80 feet

42. Shao Lin Degree 13d

Start on *Shadow Boxing* and finish on *Zero Degrees*. 80 feet

43. Organic 14b ★

Start in underclings, moving left and up steep wall to horizontal band. Join *Basra* to the top. 80 feet

44. Virga 13c ★

Tram start. Short route that moves past hard pulls, ending at anchor near horizontal band of pockets. 4 bolts, 35 feet

Jed Workman climbing *Killer* (12c).
Photo © David Anderson

45. Kingdom of Jah 12c/d ★★

Share start with *Cartoon*, but traverse even further right, then up good pockets to anchors just left of black streak. 75 feet

46. Nirvana 13a ★★

Same start as *Cartoon*, but continue right where *Cartoon* goes straight up. Long moves up a continuously steep wall. 85 feet

47. Samsara 13b ★★★

Climb *Cartoon Graveyard* to the horizontal rest, then up and right through roof. 90 feet

48. Cartoon Graveyard 12d ★★★

A0 start (at ring bolt and standard hanger) to undercling, then up right through low crux. After rest go straight up to anchors below six foot roof. The extension through the roof is *Exodus*. 80 feet

49. Exodus 13c ★★

A three-bolt extension to *Cartoon Graveyard* that adds substantially to the difficulty. 90 feet

50. Stronger Than Reason 13b/c ★

Hard thin pockets straight up from the *Killer* start bolt. Joins *Mr. Majestyk* at high horizontal. This climb is a solid 13c if done to the full *Majestyk* finish. 90 feet

51. Mr. Majestyk 13a ★★★

Up *Killer* to the end of the seam, then right through 12a crux, up corner to good rest. Punch it through steep climbing to horizontal, and up left to share *Sweet Bro* anchors. **Mrs. Majestyk** is a 12d variation that traverses right to the *Cartoon Graveyard* anchors before the crux lip moves. 90 feet

52. Sweet Bro 13a ★

Takes *Killer* to just above the roof, then moves right and up hard long moves, then over roof at top. 90 feet

53. Killer 12c ★★

A0 start (usually a fixed aider on bolt one) to gain seam, follow it left and up to juggy wall and roof above. 80 feet

54. The Successor 13b ★★

Thin moves up seam feature, then up continuous difficulties to roof at top. 80 feet

SINKS CANYON : Main Wall

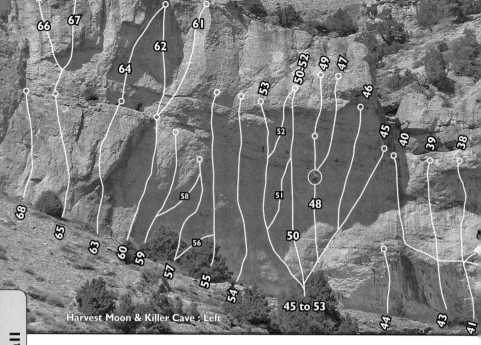

Harvest Moon & Killer Cave : Left

55. The Throne 13a ★★★

Hard crimping leads to an undercling, then long moves up headwall. 80 feet

56. Wield the Scepter 13b ★★

Starts just right of *Busload*, traverses hard undercling arch into *The Throne*, then up that route. See photo page 16. 85 feet

57. Busload of Faith 14a ★★

Hard moves from the get-go. 60 feet

58. Sister Ray 13a

Start as for *Moonstone*, but head right and join the upper section of *Busload of Faith*. 60 feet

59. Moonstone 13b ★★

Climb up hard moves to a great jug, past more hard moves, and up easier terrain. This climb follows a beautiful golden streak. 70 feet

60. Blue Moon 12a ★★

Great climbing up big flake and through overhanging terrain above to anchors after bolt six. 70 feet

61. Full Moon 12a

The original extension of *Blue Moon* which adds 60 feet of 11a climbing to the very popular, shorter version. Use caution when lowering.

62. To the Moon, Alice 12b ★

Continue straight up the wall above the lower half of *Blue Moon*, heading for the top of *Cutthroat*. This is a very high route, use care in lowering! 50 feet

63. Brown Trout 11c

Unfortunately a little wet, but good climbing through diagonal roof. 85 feet

64. Cutthroat 11d

The big leaning corner above *Brown Trout*. Use care in lowering if climbing this route from the ground; a 60 meter rope will barely get you down. 45 feet

Steve Babits climbing *Brown Trout* (11c).
Photo © David Anderson.

Harvest Moon Wall

65. Sign of the Times 11b

P1 Technical climbing up and left to chain anchor. 50 feet

66. Sign of the Times 13a ★

P2 Up black streak in headwall above chains.

Total length is 105 feet. Be careful on rappel/lower.

67. Hypernova 12b ★★★

From the end of *Sign of the Times* pitch one, climb up and right to roof then over and up shallow corner. Use caution when lowering! 105 feet

68. Powderfinger 11a ★

Follow seam to big flake, then up and over to jugs above. 6 bolts, 50 feet

69. After the Goldrush 11c ★★

Climbs thin face to easier pocketed headwall. 7 bolts, 60 feet

70. Harvest Rush 10b

An alternate start to *After the Goldrush* that traverses in from *Harvest Moon*.

71. Harvest Moon 11a ★★

Start up rightward undercling, then straight up on glassy holds. Features ring-type bolts. Continuous. 55 feet

72. Sun Spot 11d ★

Climb up slick crimps and small pockets to good holds near the top. 45 feet

73. Firecracker Kid 10b ★★

Up lieback flake, then traverse left to corner climbing. 55 feet

74. Elmo's Fish 10d ★★

Climb up shallow corner to undercling and up steep face. 60 feet

75. Pocket Calculator 12b ★

Starts just left of large bush, up thin pockets to long easier wall above. 60 feet

76. Sam I Am 9 ★★

Nice easy route up a corner to a face. Can get dirty from runoff.

77. Global Warm-Up 10c ★

Begin in small corner, and up to less steep terrain. 6 bolts, 45 feet

78. Dutch Rudder 12a ★

This climb is a techy boulder problem to easier climbing. 50 feet

79. Put Down Your Ducky 8 ★★

Exceedingly popular slab route. 80 feet

80. The Ogre 11a

Short route just right of a small gully. No photo. 30 feet

Lee Brown climbing *Harvest Moon* **(11a).**
Photo © Steve Bechtel.

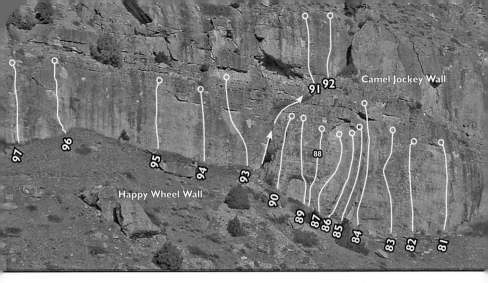

Camel Jockey Wall

81. Red Light Love 11c ★
Start on flakes, up right, then fun moves to anchor. 65 feet

82. Lost Boy 12d
Burly thin climbing. 50 feet

83. Child's Play 10c ★
Flakes to thin crux, then up and right to anchors. 55 feet

84. More Funky Than Gunky 9 ★★
Very popular crack in corner then up through small roof. 70 feet

85. Camel Jockey 13b ★
Up center of pretty wall on long moves. 60 feet

86. Sand Digger 12b ★★
Start on hard boulder problem into crack, then up steep face to hard exit moves. 65 feet

87. Wammoe 12b/c
Continuously hard moves up vertical wall. 60 feet

88. Project
89. Straight Up Crew 11c ★
Up right side of small arch, then through bulge to slab. 50 feet

90. No Self Control 10c
Thin slab climbing. 45 feet

91. Spent Rods 11b
This route and *Bad Milk* begin on the ledge up behind No Self *Control*. Climb up gully to left to reach the ledge. 35 feet

92. Bad Milk 11a
The right route on the upper ledge, this climb is the better of the two. 35 feet

93. Bones Brigade 10a
Climb up face into left-trending corner. 65 feet

94. Hunger Force 11c
Climb off flake into hard crux, then up easier moves to top. Sharp. 45 feet

95. Dogtown 9 ★
Climb a right-facing corner to big holds. 45 feet

96. Dreaming the Rasta Bus 10a ★★
Fun slab to pockets. 40 feet

97. Z-Boys 8 ★★
Follows fun flakes up a low-angle wall. 50 feet

98. Passion Party 10c
Climbs steep rock on off-balance moves. 45 feet

99. Project Wild Flower Royale
Steep prow/leaning corner problem on a steep wall. 50 feet

100. White Lotus 13c ★
Climbs steep rock on off-balance moves. 45 feet

101. Twice Baked 11c
Takes the prow right of *Happy Wheel*. 50 feet

102. Happy Wheel 10a ★
Start in well-protected corner, then move out of corner to right and up face. 45 feet

103. Where They Gonna Run When Destruction Comes? 12c ★
Up difficult face to hard high bulge. 70 feet

104. Cloud Calling 12b

Climb the dark streak up a gently overhanging wall. Traverse left to *Yellow Cake* anchors. 50 feet

105. Yellow Cake 12b

Thin moves, hard mono, and an easier top. 50 feet

106. Pet Arête 10d

Balancy arête to spicy rightward traverse at top. Shares *Yellow Cake* anchors. 50 feet

The Brisket Wall ────────────────────────

107. Pigs in Zen 10c

Very short red slab, right side. 30 feet

108. Caught Stealing 10c

Very short red slab, left side. 30 feet

109. Praying to the Aliens 10b ★

Climbs an awkward crack system to anchors just below big ledge. 35 feet

110. Rokai Corner 8 ★

Fun, easy climbing up polished corner. 40 feet

111. The Guyver 10a ★★

Follow thin seam and face to anchors near a small roof. 45 feet

112. Fine Dining 12b ★

Seams and thin edges right of *Brisket*. 45 feet

113. The Brisket 12c

Very bouldery climbing up seam, then left and up face. 45 feet

114. Angel of Mercy 11a ★

This route follows the big corner crack, then moves left to share the last half with *Guardian Angel*. 75 feet

115. Guardian Angel 12a

Thin face moves on wall left of big corner to fun headwall above. 75 feet

116. Pocket Full of Kryptonite 13b ★

This climb has been extended to the horizontal break and now has a proper two-bolt anchor. Climb 5.11 face then left and through a bulge on thuggish moves. 70 feet

117. Titanic 11b ★

Climbs left-facing corner to ledge, then through bulge and up long face above. 100 feet

118. Little Creatures 11b ★★

Traverse ledge right to the beginning of this route. Hard thin moves lead to fun, pumpy climbing above. Be careful lowering off if your rope is less than 60 meters. 85 feet

119. Peter Bopp 11a ★

Up face/seam to hard headwall. 80 feet

120. Hale Bopp 10d ★

Climbs low-angle face to progressively steeper wall. Baffling crux at top. 80 feet

121. Storm Warning 9 ★★

Climb up edges and seams to right side of bulge, then over it to a ledge and up vertical wall above. 80 feet

122. Spike n' Vein 11b ★★★

Similar to *No Impact* but with an easier slab and easier bulge. 50 feet

123. No Impact 11d ★★

Hard slab climbing leads to big moves through bulge. 50 feet

124. Searching for Jose Cuervo 12b ★★

Climb up tricky slab to bulge, trough bulge on thin pockets, then up fun headwall. 80 feet

125. Central Pillar 11a ★

Climb up tall "pillar", then past thin moves into left-facing corner feature. Up past ledge to fun headwall. 80 feet

126. Consumption 12b ★

Continuously difficult moves between small holds. 50 feet

127. Project The Sting

Very thin crimping on a nearly blank wall. 50 feet

128. War Party 12b

Low crux in seam, leads to easier climbing. 50 feet

129. Blushing Crow 12c ★★

Shares start with *White Heat*, moves right and up long moves between good pockets. 55 feet

Rio Rose climbing *White Heat* (12d).
Photo © David Anderson.

130. White Heat 12d ★★

Start in small left-facing corner, the up and left to huecos. Hard moves from these lead to easier climbing. 55 feet

131. Project Acid Ranger

Looks really hard. Thin crimps, long moves. 50 feet

132. Mono a Mono 13a ★

Long moves between monos. 50 feet

133. Dime Time 13a

Hateful crimps up vertical wall. 50 feet

134. Fun, Fun, Joy, Joy 10b ★

Climbs up corner then out onto face to the right. 50 feet

135. Shortie Sortie 10c

Up center of slab right of Addiction Wall. 40 feet

136. Dewalt's Challenge 11d
Steep climbing up flakes and edges. Tends to collect a bit of dirt from runoff. 25 feet

137. The Black Hole 12d ★
Hard steep moves past obvious "black hole" pocket. 35 feet

138. White Dwarf 12c ★★
Continuous hard moves up bulging wall. 40 feet

139. Corner Drug 11a ★★
The chalked up corner climb. Pumpy. 55 feet

140. I Want a New Drug 12c ★
Climb the first 3 bolts of *Corner Drug*, then step left on good holds. Follow 4 bolts up the steep face above.

141. Drug Enemy 11d ★★
Climbs *Corner Drug* to third bolt, then traverses left on jugs to finish on *Public Enemy*. 65 feet

142. Public Enemy 12c ★
Climb up thin seam to good rest, then through short high crux at top. 70 feet

143. The Gathering 13b/c ★★
Steep climbing on crimps. 70 feet

144. Pretty Hate Machine 13b ★★★
Directly behind the big tree. Long, hard moves. 75 feet

145. Dogs of War 13b ★★
Hard barn-door moves to crimp crux. 75 feet

146. Addiction 12c ★★★
Climb up and right on crimps to a good rail, then up long moves to a final slab crux. 70 feet

147. Surplus Fusion Reaction 13a ★★
Steep face left of *Addiction*, crimps and small pockets. 65 feet

148. Soul Finger 11a ★★
Starts as for *Mezzmerie*, but moves right and up corner. 55 feet

149. Mezzmerie 12c
Climbs up seam to small ledge, then out left onto face. 45 feet

150. Go West, Young Man 7 ★★★
Climb left-arcing crack. 45 feet

151. Soup Sandwich 8 ★
Slab to *Go West* anchors. 40 feet

152. A Beautiful Life 9 ★★
Follow flakes and seam up slab. Named in memory of Jim Ratz. 45 feet

153. Black Celebration 11b
On high wall above and left of Addiction wall. Black streak. 30 feet

Wendy Davis climbing *Dogs of War* (13b).
Photo © David Anderson.

The Citadel Wall

154. The Earth Died Screaming 12b
Easier climbing leads to long hard headwall moves. 75 feet

155. The Stronghold of Decay 12c ★
Work up thin, sometimes dirty moves, past a few really cool holds. 75 feet

156. Citadel of Hope 12b ★★★
Climb up and right on good holds to horizontal, then up through twisty, fun moves. 75 feet

157. Divine Intervention 13b ★
Climb *Citadel* to horizontal, then up and left on very small holds. 75 feet

158. West of Hell 13b ★★
Lower-angled face to crimpy headwall. Ends beneath large block. 75 feet

159. Paladin 12a ★

Stout crimping leads to long headwall moves. 75 feet

160. Tel Aviv Miracle 12b ★★

Relentless crimping leads to a good rest, then a tricky finishing move. 50 feet

161. Right About Now 11c ★★

Hard face climbing to BIG jug, then up steep wall to easy slab finish. 70 feet

162. Funk Soul Brother 12a ★

Easier vertical face leads to horizontal break with tricky climbing above. 70 feet

163. Blood Brother 11a ★★★

Climb ramp to vertical face that leads to slightly overhanging seam. (see photo pages 10-11). 75 feet

164. Wide Awake Zombie 12b

Climbs face just left of *Blood Brother*. Difficult to stay left of *Blood Brother* at crux. 75 feet

165. Fun Planet 10a ★

Follows slab to high right-facing dihedral on left side of Citadel Wall. 70 feet

166. Biltong Rides Tornado 10c ★★

Just right of *Fat Boys*, fun climbing up steep wall. 50 feet

167. Fat Boys Skip School 11a

Begins on ledge system reached by scrambling up from right. Climbs up flakes and pockets to high crux. 50 feet

Kirk Billings climbing *Citadel of Hope* (12b).
Photo © David Anderson.

168. Value Pack 12b
Climbs up ledge systems to high crux on wall right of *Postcards* flake. 80 feet

169. Project Anchor bolts only.

170. Postcards From the Edge 11d
Follow short arête on detached block to anchors. 30 feet

171. Mutt and Jeff 11b ★★
Shares the start chimney of *Heaven Can Wait*, then moves right and up well-protected face above. 80 feet

172. Heaven Can Wait 11c ★★
A chimney to a leftward traverse joining *The Heavens*. 75 feet

173. The Heavens 13b ★
Hard moves lead to a good rest, then 5.11 climbing to the top. 75 feet

174. First Responder 13b ★★
Thin climbing up to scoop, then up, up, up to high crux. 90 feet

175. Murgatroid 12a ★★
Hard edge climbing leads to a good rest in a scoop, followed by easier, but continuous climbing above. 80 feet

176. Angry Bob 12c ★
Climbs crimps up gold streak. 60 feet

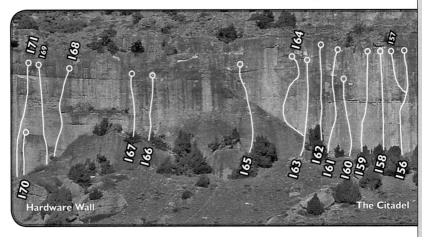

Hardware Wall The Citadel

Hardware Wall

177. Upheaval 13b ★★
Long pulls lead up and right toward *Angry Bob*. 70 feet

178. Mark 13 13a ★★
Follows seams to long reaches between crimps. 70 feet

179. Software 12c
A direct start to the top of *Hardware*, usually a bit damp. 65 feet

180. Hardware 12a ★★
Climb up thin crack to a rightward traverse, then up easier climbing to top.
Chalked sidepulls mark the start. 65 feet

181. Jill 12d ★
A desperate crimp move leads to easier climbing above. 65 feet

182. Moe 12b/c ★★
Begin in a left-facing lieback with lots of chalk. Large crimps and jugs.
Very fun, but with a couple of somewhat greasy holds at the top. 60 feet

183. Shades 12d ★★
Steep small crimps, continuous. 60 feet

184. The Zone 13b ★
Crimp your way to the top. 60 feet

185. Slippery People 12b
Poor. "Trouty" damp rock makes for a disappointing climb. 60 feet

186. Milkman 13a ★★
Bouldery movement on edges and small pockets. 60 feet

187. The Evil One 13a ★
Climb right on "ramp" hold, then past savage moves to anchor. 60 feet

188. No Left Ear 10d ★★ or 11d
Up well-protected juggy face to anchors, or continue through very hard roof. 75 feet

189. Whipperly Wamberly Walk 11b ★★
Climb up ledges to a small overhang, then up tough moves to jugs. Follow good holds up and over the high roof. 75 feet

190. Apple City Quick Step 11b
Up slab to interesting roof. 75 feet

Face Dancer Wall

191. Billie Idol 8
Climbs up the easy south face of the leaning pillar (5.4), then up good pockets on the main wall above. 70 feet

192. Kamiakin 10b ★
Start on blocky ledge just left of the leaning pillar. 65 feet

193. No More Heroes 10c
Hard low to easy climbing up slab. 60 feet

194. Fallen Idol 11b
Hard move low to easy slab above. 65 feet

195. Wind River Rose 11a
Begins just above jumbled boulders, a bit dirty. 70 feet

196. Wicker Man 11b

Sharp climbing. Go right at top. 75 feet

197. Eros 10d ★★

Climb up and right on rails and pockets. 85 feet

198. Face Dancer 11b ★★★

Popular route leads up big flake/slab to vertical wall with glassy pockets. 85 feet

199. Winds of War 10c ★★

Start up ramp, then follow sustained moves to anchors. 85 feet

200. Diemos 10d ★★

Up gray slab, then through fun moves to a right-facing corner near the top. 85 feet

Photo © Ken Driese.

201. Blessed Saint Yabo 11c ★★

Begins with the same bouldery move as *Stone Seed*, but moves straight up where *Stone Seed* traverses left. 50 feet

202. Stone Seed 11d ★ (2 short pitches)

Hard moves off pointy flakes at bottom to rail, then traverse left and up to anchors. A second, easier, pitch leads higher. 80 feet

203. Calling Saint Fiacre 11c ★

Climb small pillar/corner to hard moves that lead into the end of *Stone Seed*. 60 feet

204. Skinny Fat Man 12d ★

Takes the gray steak on the rightmost side of the Moss Cave. Technical. 6 bolts, 65 feet

Steve Bechtel in the Moss Cave.

Moss Cave

205. Smoke Shapes 13d/14a ★★
Jump start to monos up streak. 55 feet

206. Traveling Menagerie 14b
This climb does the *Smoke Shapes* start then traverses low across the cave to finish on *Confession of a Mask*.

207. Project The Man They Couldn't Hang

208. Dealer Calls 14a ★★
This is the winch start to the line originally envisioned as "The Man." Clip a bolt at the lip of the cave near an obvious undercling flake, winch up, and go to work.

209. Confession of a Mask 12d ★★★
A0 Tram start leads to long moves between generally good holds.

210. The Abortionist 13c ★
Do the A0 tram start for *Confession of a Mask*, but climb left and into the top of *Pogey Bait*.

211. Project Undertow
Climb from *Confession* tram start all the way along the undercling crack to finish on *Mr. Gorsky*.

212. Pogey Bait 13c ★
This is the second line from the left in the Moss Cave. Boulder crux to easier climbing above.

213. Taking The Pythons For A Walk 13c ★★
Start *Pogey Bait*, then traverse left to *Gorsky* at the undercling.

214. Aces Wild 13a ★★
Start with the first three bolts of *Mr. Gorsky*, then move right and finish on *Pogey Bait*.

215. Good Luck Mr. Gorsky 13c ★★
A0 Tram start. Hard pulls on continuously steep wall.

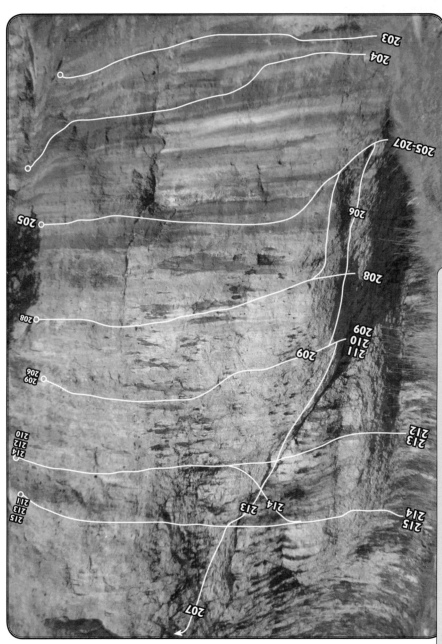

216. Touchy Feely 11d

Climb up the left side of a white streak, about 50 feet after the trail exits the small "forest". 70 feet

Purple Galaxy Wall

217. Bush Fire 12a ★

Good climb up rust streak on right side of clean wall. 50 feet

218. Crowheart 12b/c ★★

Good route up center of wall. Same anchors as *Macumba*. 50 feet

219. Macumba 11d

Thin and sharp face, just right of *Southpaw* crack. 50 feet

220. Southpaw 10c ★★

Climb a left-leaning undercling crack, exiting onto face above. 50 feet

221. Monkey in the White House 12b ★

Follows light-colored rock from top of flake/ledge. 45 feet

222. Cheese Wheel 12d/13a

Follow a dirty and razor sharp line behind a tree, trending left at the start. Originally 12b, breaking rock continues to up the difficulty. 50 feet

223. Purple Galaxy 12a ★★★

A hard opening sequence leads to a good rest; then up tough moves to a horizontal. Either lower from anchors here (11d, 80 feet) or continue three more bolts to the top. 100 feet

224. Project

225. Aqualung 11c

Climb a big left-facing corner and up the face above. 60 feet

226. Gongoozled 11d ★★

Continuous tricky moves, then through a hard bulge at the top. 85 feet

227. Grabbing Greta 11c ★

Start in a left-facing corner, moves left to difficult moves on a slab, then climb through a bulge near the top.

228. Parts and Labor 11b

Take the slab up to steeper climbing, then through a small roof at the top. 90 feet

Achin' for Bootie Wall ────────────

229. Waiting on a Friend 11b ★★

A difficult entry move leads to fun jug pulling and a small bulge above. 80 feet

230. Smell My Finger 11d ★★

Climb face right of *Achin'* to crack feature at top. Pumpy. 90 feet

231. Achin' for Bootie 12a ★★★

Climb up right-facing corner to a small ledge with a chain bolt. Move straight up the center of the face to a high crux. 95 feet

232. Cavity Search 11d ★

Slab to lieback crack, then hard bulge before headwall. 90 feet

233. Picture of Industry 11c ★★

Climb a crack feature up to a bulge, then through it and up to anchors near a small bush. 85 feet

234. Ride the Apocalypse 12b ★

Climb up blocky rock behind a tree to a very hard move, followed by 5.10 climbing to the anchors. 70 feet

235. Brrravery 12b ★

Up right-trending seam and then up clean face above. 65 feet

236. Opal 12a

Up the face just left of a small corner, then through a mini roof to anchor on the arête above. 65 feet

237. Renaissance Man 8

Up prow/slab on sharp rock. Poorly bolted. If not for *Spragglepuss*, this would be the worst rout on the whole crag. 60 feet

238. Bust A Nut 11b ★★

Climb up small pillar to discontinuous cracks. Follow cracks and good moves to anchor below the large square-cut roof. 50 feet

239. Bump-N-Grind 12a

Follows deceptive prow to anchors below large square-cut roof. 50 feet

240. Spragglepuss 10c

Low angle climbing behind large pine. A turd. 45 feet

241. Combustification 11a ★

Double cracks. 55 feet

SINKS CANYON : Main Wall

The Wilds

242. The Physical 12c ★

Hard moves to groove, continuing difficulty, steep top out. 6 bolts, 50 feet

243. Snap Back Relax 12d/13a ★

Boulder problem start to easier moves. 50 feet

244. Wicked Garden 9

Chossy gully. 55 feet

245. Aggressive Perfector 13b ★

A boulder problem to a large hueco, then 5.12 rambling above. 60 feet

246. Savages 13a ★★

Good thin climbing up nice wall, just left of obvious hueco. 50 feet

247. The Wilds 12a ★★
Start up small left-facing corner, then up hard moves above.

248. Get on With It 12b ★★
Hard, thin climbing. Technical.

249. Sandman 10c ★★
Up thin right-facing flake system to steeper wall above.

250. Tooth Fairy 10c ★
Techy face climbing, starting in small groove. Continuous.

251. Ankle Biter 10d
Up low angle rock to rightward traverse near top.

252. Candyman 10d ★
The leftmost route on the wall. Climb up easy left-facing corner/ flake system to ledge (5.5), then up steep wall above. 60 feet

253. Earth A.D. 9 ★
Slab with jugs and nice moves to ledge. 40 feet

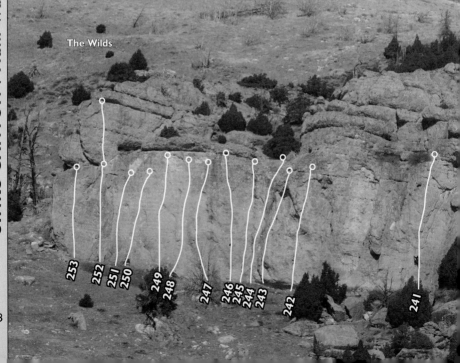

SINKS CANYON : Main Wall

254. Project Girly
Steep wall left of the *German Girl* arête. 4 bolts, 35 feet

255. German Girl 12a
The steep and cool looking overhanging arête. Sharper than Ken Jennings. 35 feet

256. Burly 11d ★★
A semi-classic. Jug haul it up the west face right of the arête. 40 feet

257. Boys From Brazil 11c ★
Steep corner and face right of *Burly*. 40 feet

258. Isolate and Dominate 10c ★
This climb takes the black streak right of *Boys from Brazil*. Good moves. 35 feet

259. Full Irations 12a ★
The left route on the SE face, start off boulder to reachy moves. 30 feet

260. Zion Train 12b ★★
Good pockets up center of face. 35 feet

261. Steel Pulse 11a
Right of *Zion Train*, a tricky and sharp route. 35 feet

262. EZ Up 10c
Hard start leads to easy climbing above. 40 feet

263. When I Hang My Boots to Rest 12b
Bouldery lead version of the old toprope "Darksides." 30 feet

264. Original Route 9
Bolted corner on north side. 35 feet

265. Crack Fox 11a ★
Step off the boulder and pull. 30 feet

266. Girls of Rock Springs 11d no photo
Filthy choss tucked away in the boulders uphill from Squaretop.

SINKS CANYON : Main Wall

APPROACH (Squaretop Boulder)

The Squaretop Boulder is best reached via parking at the Fairfield Hill road (0.4 miles past the main parking area). See page 152 for details.

South Side

North Side

Wave of Mutilation Boulder

See photo on page 110-111 for an overview location of this boulder.

> ### APPROACH (Wave of Mutilation Boulder)
>
> The Wave of Mutilation Boulder can be reached by walking the Addiction Trail to the first switchback, then angling downhill toward the road and around to the south face of the rock.

267. Monkey Gone To Heaven 14b ★★

The left route on the Wave of Mutilation Boulder. Monos, etc. 25 feet

268. Wave of Mutilation 13c ★★

Long moves between good pockets. Steep! 30 feet

SINKS CANYON : Fairfield Hill ─────────

The Fairfield Hill cliff is the westernmost developed dolomite cliff in Sinks Canyon. Fairfield has always been the black sheep of Sinks Canyon climbing. Although development here has paralleled that of the Main Wall, it has received only a fraction the traffic. Development here has included several climbers; but, well over half of the 100+ climbs were established by Bob Branscomb. His efforts, and the efforts of Ed Delong, Paul Piana, Dave Doll, and a few others have created one of the finest crags in Wyoming.

DRIVE TIME: 15 minutes from Lander

HIKE: 20 to 30 minutes uphill

SUN EXPOSURE: Sunny until 4 p.m.

SEASON: Spring, Fall, Summer evenings

LENGTH: 40 to 80 feet

FAIRFIELD ROUTE COUNT by GRADE

<5.9 : 23 — **5.10** : 28 — **5.11** : 26 — **5.12** : 18 — **5.13** : 4

PARKING & APPROACH (Fairfield Hill)

Drive up canyon 3 miles from the "Entering Sinks Canyon State Park" sign, and take the two-track on the right. If you have a low clearance vehicle, it may be best to park just off the pavement and walk. Follow this road for three-quarters of a mile and park. Walk up the very rough 4WD road above for about 250 yards to a right-hand trail marked by two large cairns. Follow this long diagonal all the way to the right end of the Fairfield Hill cliff. From here a climbers' trail leads back west (left) along the base.

Routes are described from right to left.

This is also a good approach trail for the left end of the Sinks Main Wall. An obvious trail connects the Fairfield and Main Walls near the top of the long diagonal of the Fairfield approach trail.

---

1. French Blow 10c ★
Overhanging line on east side of pillar

2. Hieroglyphic 11c ★
The right route on the pinnacle; rightmost route on Fairfield Hill. Takes center of steep face. No photo. 55 feet

3. Kissing Marilyn Monroe 11c
On left side of the arête of "pinnacle" formation; turn arête at bolt four. 50 feet

4. They Shoot Horses 11b ★
On face of pinnacle; begins with left-hand sidepulls. 50 feet

5. Con's West Right 6
The right-hand slab uphill and west of the pinnacle. 25 feet

6. Con's West Left 10a
The left slab. 3 bolts, 25 feet

7. Afterthought 10b
Slab with long chain anchor. 30 feet

8. Apostrophe 10a
Shares bolt one with *Treats*. 40 feet

9. Treats 9 ★
Harder than the others, but really fun. 40 feet

10. Revenge of the Pygmy Sex God 8 ★
Short, but fun.

11. Realm of the Venusian Sex Pygmies 7
Nice easy climb.

12. West of Venus 7
Nice slab. 45 feet

13. Say Hello To Geronimo 10b ★★
Through little bulge to easy slab above. 6 bolts, 50 feet

14. A Piolet for Leon 10d ★
Thin and tricky face climbing. 50 feet

15. Che 11d ★
Similar to previous route. 50 feet

16. Leon Trotsky's Hair 11c ★
Thin crimping up nice face. 60 feet

17. Sorta Maybe Kinda Wild 10b ★★
Corner to face traverse right. Shares anchors with *Leon Trotsky's Hair*. 60 feet

SINKS CANYON : Fairfield Hill

East Wall : Left Side

18. Leslie's Arête 12a/b
Devious arête with three bolts.

19. Big Bambu 11b
Long moves past 3 bolts on slightly overhanging wall. 35 feet

20. Blind 11d
Vertical wall with big flakes. 75 feet

21. Restless Natives 12d ★
Dark streak right of arches. Start by stick clipping the second bolt. Climb up and right of the bolt line to bolt 3, then follow the bolt line. The direct start would be *substantially* harder. 75 feet

22. Pistol Whipped 12a ★
Boulder problem down low (as usual) to a techy slab. 60 feet

23. Devilution 12b
Low boulder problem to climbing on pods. A bit dirty. 55 feet

24. Nimord 11a
A hard start in a corner leads to a leftward move, then up easier sustained climbing. Just right of *Presence*. 55 feet

25. Presence 10d ★
Dark wall starting near grey bushes. 50 feet

26. Houses of the Holy 10b ★★
Good slab route, starts behind junipers. 50 feet

27. Second Helping 10a ★★★
Face between *Physical Graffiti* and *Houses of the Holy*. 7 bolts

28. Physical Graffiti 11a ★
Tricky climbing. 45 feet

29. Your Own Private Idaho 10c ★
Good slab climbing beneath big boulder at rim. 45 feet

30. L, L, & L 8
Leftmost route on white slab. 35 feet

31. Meadow Rock TRs
Several short top ropes between Central and Right sectors.

Beef Pudding Wall

32. World On A String 11b
Tricky and sharp. 40 feet

33. Hanoi Jane's Video Workout 11a
Up face and into crack with tree. 40 feet

34. Brave Like Old John Wayne 11d ★
Tech climbing on left end of black vertical wall. 40 feet

35. Beef Pudding 12c ★
Right route on east-facing block. 40 feet

36. Zebra Cakes 12b ★★
Left side of east-facing block. 40 feet

Fairfield Central Wall

37. Straight, No Chaser 10b
Climbs long arête/flake feature. 60 feet

38. Exile on Main Street 12a ★
Sustained climbing on small holds. 65 feet

39. Electric Fence 12b ★★
Up clean white face and through the high bulges. 75 feet

40. Hellzapoppin 11d ★★
Start in right-facing corner, up clean wall, and finish through bulge at top. 70 feet

41. Nobody's Fault But Mine 10b
Good short route. 35 feet

42. I Wish I Was A Catfish 10c
Similar to nearby routes. 40 feet

43. Atom Tan 10c ★
A good and techy climb. 40 feet

44. Jump Jim Crow 11b ★
Continuous difficulty. 40 feet

45. Have Mercy 10c ★
Tricky slab. 40 feet

46. Visualize Whirled Peas 10b ★★
Another short route, really fun. 35 feet

47. Last Trip To Tulsa 8 ★
Short and fun. 35 feet

48. Coyote Delight 7
Decent and cleaner than most Fairfield routes. 40 feet

49. Slave to History 10a ★
This is a short face on good rock. 40 feet

50. Uncle Meat 8
Sporty but good holds. 40 feet

51. Youth Culture Killed My Dog 9 ★
Best of these routes. 45 feet

52. Born Cross-Eyed 10a ★
Left-trending slab route. 45 feet

53. Screaming Trees 11a ★
Challenging and sporty route just right of *Chainsaw Willy*, starts behind juniper. 50 feet

54. Chainsaw Willy 10d ★★
Climb left-leaning crack to face above. 50 feet

55. Touch of Gray 10c ★★
Well-protected route just left of small prow. 45 feet

56. Alan Shepard Goes to Space 11b ★
Starts in overlaps right of big juniper. 65 feet

57. Saucerful of Secrets 11d ★★
Good route up clean vertical wall. End at 3-bolt anchor. 60 feet

The Doll Face

58. Our Barbies, Ourselves 12a ★
Improbable line up overhanging wall. 70 feet

59. Doll Parts 11d ★
Climb up steep terrain and then up right side of corner. 70 feet

60. Doll Face 13b ★★
Curving line on right side of clean steep wall. 70 feet

61. My Dying Bride 12d ★
Takes the left side of the beautiful steep face. 65 feet

62. Tweedle Dum 6
The right short face. 25 feet

63. Tweedle Dee 5
Left of two short faces. 25 feet

64. Cheaper Than Religion 10a ★★
This long ramble is well protected and fun.

Spooky Tooth Wall

65. Kashmir 11a
Takes arête and face to disappointingly low anchors. 45 feet

66. Viatameen H 12d ★★
Sprint route on nice steep prow. 35 feet

67. A Dream of Least Weasels 12b ★★
Thin holds, great rock. 35 feet

68. Save a Prayer For Lefty 13b ★
Follow a left leaning flake to hard high face moves. 35 feet

69. Shadowline 11b
Tricky climbing up rounded arête. 40 feet

70. Manifest Destiny 10a
Great climbing for a little route. 30 feet

71. Axis of Weasel 12a ★★
Entry crux leads to easier ground on pretty rock. 35 feet

72. Weasels Ripped My Flesh 12b ★
Hard start leads to super nice jugs up a black streak. 40 feet

73. Moveable Feast 9 ★
Up lieback flake. 45 feet

74. New World Ordor 7 ★
The corner. 45 feet

75. The Great Deceiver 11a ★★
Pretty reddish face right of the big tooth. 50 feet

76. Spooky Tooth 7
Flake climb. Right side. The left side of this flake is 5.5 and is done with gear. 4 bolts, 45 feet

77. Hand on the Torch 10a ★
A tricky entry sets you up for fun climbing above. 35 feet

78. Take Some Petrol, Darling 8 ★
A nice, more moderate addition to the wall. 35 feet

79. Revolution is Evolution 7 ★★
Another good route. 35 feet

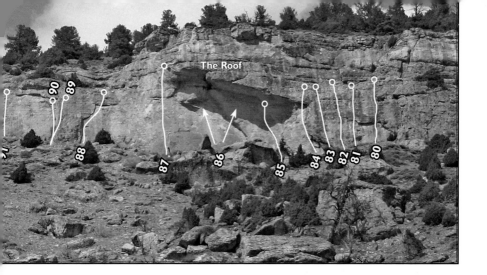

The Roof

The Roof is about 50 yards left of the route *Spooky Tooth*.

80. Black Sunday 10c
A red and black streaked crack. 40 feet

81. More Cowbell 10b ★
A jump start leads to less jumping. Stick clip. 40 feet

82. Swift 11a
This face is left of a small roof, climbs technical black rock. 45 feet

83. Driller's Delight 11d
Up left leaning crack feature to vertical climbing above. 45 feet

84. The Abortion 11d
Thin face moves to turn big roof at its very right side. 50 feet

85. Zeb 9
A left-arching crack, 5 feet left of *The Abortion*. 40 feet

86. Projects
Roof projects.

87. The Brotherhood 11d ★★
This climbs takes the long steep wall above two huge blocks at the left end of the roof. 90 feet

88. Blah, Blah, Blah 10d ★★

This cool climb takes a corner to an undercling traverse right, then up the face above. 45 feet

89. Teanagers from Mars 8 ★

Climb the rounded prow feature. A bit sharp. 40 feet

90. Devil Lock 6

Up a corner to exit moves on big pockets. 40 feet

91. The Plague 12d

Clean face just right of red rock. 3 bolts to chain anchor. 40 feet

92. Sensor 11c

Dark wall, thin slab. 3 bolts, 35 feet

93. Some Like Another Chance 10a ★

Short rute behind some junipers. Fun.

94. Tenth Monkey 9

Just left of *Some Like Another Chance*, just not as good.

95. Only As Pretty As You Feel 8 ★

Another route on cool pockets that takes longer to read the description than to climb. 30 feet

96. Wyoming Hair Disaster 8 ★

A good climb, parallels *Only As Pretty As You Feel.*

The Bubble Wall

The Bubble Wall is about 75 yards left of the others.

97. Blessed Black Wings 13a ★★

Climbs a prominent black streak on the right side of The Bubble and is the longest route in the area. 65 feet

98. Fizzle Doubt 12c ★★

Up overhanging face right of the main "bubble." 50 feet

99. Sheepeater 13a ★

Through center of bulge.

100. Don Ho 12b ★★★

Takes left side of bulge. 50 feet

101. Afternoon Delight 12b

Leftmost route on the wall, bouldery pocket climbing.

SINKS CANYON : Fairfield Hill

SINKS CANYON : Granite Crags

The granite crags of Sinks Canyon are a microscopic version of the Wind Rivers to the west. Climbers have long visited these cliffs, but only recently have they seen concentrated activity. As early as the 1960s, climbers were establishing lines on the Z-Crack Wall and the Granite Buttress. More recently, in the fall of 2010, the Lander Area's hardest boulder problem was established on a block at the base of these walls. The climbs here range from easy multi-pitch scrambles to 5.14 projects.

These crags are best in spring and fall, though their south-facing aspect makes many of the lines climbable in winter. Summer afternoons can be pleasant at the Joint and Sancuary, as these walls start catching shade around 2pm.

The cliffs are described as you approach them from the Bruce's Parking Area. All three major areas are visible from the parking lot. The Joint is the steep and streaked wall closest to the road. The Granite Buttress is the huge rounded dome that sits a half-mile further up the trail. The Sanctuary is made up of the broken cliffs between.

Granite Crags from Bruce's Parking Lot

Granite Buttress

The Sancutary

The Joint

DRIVE TIME: 15 minutes from Lander

HIKE: 15 to 20 minutes uphill

SUN EXPOSURE: Sunny until 2 p.m. most of the year

SEASON: Spring, Fall, and Summer evenings

LENGTH: 40 to 150 feet

GRANITE CRAGS ROUTE COUNT by GRADE

<5.8 : 16 — 5.9 : 7 — 5.10 : 12 — 5.11 : 16 — 5.12 : 14 — 5.13 : 8

Granite Crags Overview

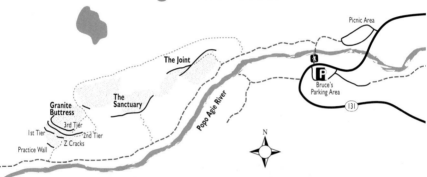

The Joint, as seen from Bruce's Parking Area.

The Fun House, 11c

Ledge

Main Wall

Right Side

The Joint is the first of the granite crags along the Middle Fork Trail, 10 minutes from Bruce's Parking Area. It is best recognized by the tall black-streaked wall that sits at the center of the crag. The main concentration of routes is on the steep, lower third of this wall. Routes exist both to the left and right of this main sector, and several potential lines exist on the upper reaches of the wall. At this time, the only route that goes all the way up is *The Fun House*, which is accessed by climbing any of the lower routes or by traversing in from the right on a wide, sloping ledge.

PARKING & APPROACH (The Joint)

The Joint is reached by parking at the "Bruce's Parking Area" just after the road crosses the river (4.2 miles from the canyon entrance). There are toilets at the Parking Area. Cross the road to the foot bridge and cross the river. Head up canyon about 5 minutes along the Middle Fork Trail. The cliff is visible for the entire approach. About 200 feet after passing the last electrical pole along the trail, angle up right and scramble to the cliff via talus slopes. Cairns mark most of this path.

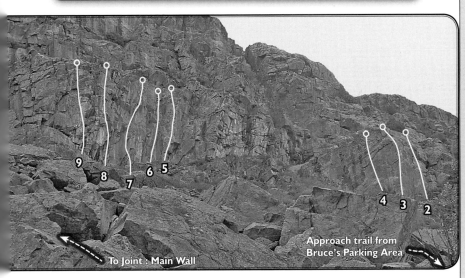

To Joint : Main Wall

Approach trail from Bruce's Parking Area

1. Moon Over Dog Street 8 no photo

This is a short face climb to a splitter hand crack 50 feet right of *1,000 Churches*.

2. 1,000 Churches 10d ★
Seams and edges. 4 bolts, 40 feet

3. Ambro-Agie 12a ★★
Arête with 4 bolts. 35 feet

4. Obscured by Clowns 11b ★★
Beautiful smooth face with great edges. 5 bolts, 40 feet

5. Slick Fifty 12a
Arête on slick red rock. 5 bolts, 45 feet

6. Ziggurat 11d ★★
Dihedral on slick rock to ledges. 4 bolts, 45 feet

7. The Rift 12b ★★
Shallow corner on red wall to ledges above. 5 bolts, 45 feet

8. Bluebeard 11d ★★★
White corner with roof to steep juggy climbing above. 5 bolts, 50 feet

9. Mr. Big Shot 11a ★★★
Steep wall with seam. 6 bolts, 50 feet

10. Open Project TS Headwall Arête
This is the last local project Todd worked on before his death.

11. Project
12. The Fun House 11c ★★
Starts on ledge at one-third height, up to summit. 100 feet

13. Soft Option 9
Up easy corner to ledge, then up corner. 3 bolts, 40 feet

14. Kid Gloves 11c ★★
Up hard face past small ledge to fun steep moves. 4 bolts, 40 feet

15. Broken Heroes 13a ★
Small corner to bulge, then up smooth face above. 5 bolts, 40 feet

16. Big Smoke 11c ★★
Liebacks and jugs lead to a hard exit move. 4 bolts, 40 feet

17. Get Wacky 12b ★
Seam climb on black streak. 4 bolts, 40 feet

SINKS CANYON : Granite

x : running belay bolts along the "Fun House" ledge.

18. Bad Brain 13d ★★
Hard bouldery moves with the famous undercling crimp. 4 bolts, 45 feet

19. Full Tilt 13b ★★
Follows seam to hard top moves. 5 bolts, 40 feet

20. Project

21. Kilodeer 10a
Up groove past 4 bolts to anchor at ledge - 40 feet. The corner above is 5.11 and is protected with small cams and wires.

22. October Sky 13a ★
Start as for *Kilodeer*, moving left and up prow after low anchor. Tricky. 100 feet

23. I'm Ron Burgundy? 12a ★
Up deceptively overhanging wall on large holds to turn small roof on the right. 8 bolts, 55 feet

24. Twelfth Labor 11c ★
Corner with seam to steep headwall. 55 feet

25. Oral History 12a ★
Start up difficult arête, then turn a tricky roof before hitting the easy climbing. 6 bolts, 50 feet

The Sanctuary

This is the nice group of buttresses between the Joint Wall and the main Granite Buttress. Although this area has seen sporadic use from climbers for several years, it wasn't until 2006 that routes were developed in earnest by John Hennings. Following in John's footsteps, Tom Rangitsch and BJ Tilden led the charge for new routes in this area. A sanctuary from both the occasional wind and from the relentless pockets of the dolomite, this is a great alternative to Lander's other crags. Routes are described from left to right.

PARKING & APPROACH (The Sanctuary)

The Sanctuary is reached by parking at the "Bruce's Parking Area" just after the road crosses the river (4.2 miles from the canyon entrance). There are toilets at the Parking Area. Cross the road to the foot bridge and cross the river. Head up canyon about 10 minutes along the Middle Fork Trail. After passing the Joint and the major boulder field below it, the trail leads into an open, sage-covered field. Walk through this field for a very short distance, then angle uphill toward the crag. This is the first section of cliff past the Joint, and is only separated from that crag by a few hundred feet of broken rock and gullies.

Upper Tier

1. Smirk 11d ★

This route is the leftmost on the wall. Start just left of a low roof. 45 feet

2. Stiff Upper Lip 13a ★★

Share start with *Smirk*. Climb up and right through a small roof and then along a seam. 45 feet

3. The Brown Arête 11b

Third route from the left, the name says it all. 50 feet

4. Backbone of the West 12b ★★

This black-and-white arête is left-facing. Really fun. 45 feet

5. No Name Crack 11b ★★

This is the splitter crack. The 5.11 ends at a ledge with a bolt. The roof above might or might not have been done at 5.12. 35 feet, small cams and wires.

The Sanctuary, Left

6. Remember a Day 8

This is the dark, wide crack to the right. As recommendable as a Susan Sontag novel. 60 feet

7. Big Pink 8

Another wide and fun adventure. Shares anchor with *Obscured by Cloud*. 40 feet

8. Obscured by Cloud 10b ★★

This is a west-facing red slab (just right of the two great wide cracks!) A good route. An extension, called "Nimbus" is 5.10 with one point of aid. 40 feet

9. Time and Materials 12c/d ★

This is the leftmost climb on the steep "Foundation Wall." A low crux leads to long moves on easier ground. 45 feet

10. Foundation 12b/c ★★★

The best route on this wall, considered to be one of the best of the grade in the whole area. 45 feet

11. Empire 12b ★★

Little brother to *Foundation*.

12. The Seldon Plan 11b ★

On the right end of the main Foundation wall, just left of broken rock on bigger holds. The warm-up for harder routes. 45 feet

13. Terminus 12a ★

This climb takes the black arête right of the previous wall.

14. The Left Jewel of Mr. Texas 10c

A V3-ish move leads to 5.10 climbing. The leftmost route on the cube-like Zirconia Boulder. This is up a wide ramp about 200 feet right of the Foundation Wall.

15. The Right Jewel of Mr. Texas 10a ★★

The right-hand slab in the Zirconia Boulder's west face. 40 feet

16. Rimfire 13b ★★

This is the steep southwest arête on the Zirconia Boulder

17. Centerfire 13d ★★★

This is the overhanging center.

18. Cornered and Cleaved 12d ★

Climb a corner, then traverse crack left to *Centerfire* finish.

19. Gemini Cracks 8 ★

Parallel cracks on a small pillar feature about 75 feet right of the Zirconia Boulder. 60 feet

20. Going, Going, Gone 11c

Bolts and thin protection up a clean slab.

21. Bullwinkle 10b ★

Slab with bolts and thin protection. 45 feet

Lower Tier

22. Monument To What? 10a ★

A short climb on a clean wall.

23. Pigs in Zen 10a ★

This is a right-facing corner on clean stone. 40 feet

24. Secret Slab 9 ★★

Four bolts plus gear to anchors. 40 feet

25. The Lathe of Heaven 12a ★ no picture

About 150 feet right of the *Secret Slab* is a very obvious overhanging arête feature. This is the route.

The Sancturary, Right

APPROACH (Granite Buttress)

The Granite Buttress is the huge dome-like crag that sits approximately one mile up canyon from the road. It is reached by parking at the "Bruce's Parking Area" just after the road crosses the river (4.2 miles from the canyon entrance). There are toilets at the Parking Area. Cross the road to the foot bridge and cross the river. Head up canyon about 3 minutes, looking for a faint climbers' path that heads uphill to the right before you reach the rocky outcrops east of the Joint. Follow this switchbacking path to the top of the hill, then take it west, above the crags of the Joint and Sanctuary. Once on top of the hill, the going is pretty easy.

After 15-20 minutes of hiking, small granite outcroppings will appear to your left (between you and the river). Walk toward these rocks on the climbers' path, and find a route down between a slab and a steep west-facing wall. There is a short, silly bolt ladder on this wall, which serves as a good point of reference. Hike down the gully at the base of this wall, looking to your right (west) for the "tier" of the Buttress you'd like to reach.

Granite Buttress

This buttress is the large dome-like feature seen up-canyon from Bruce's parking lot. This buttress consists of great Wind River granite, and is divided horizontally into three distinct tiers. In fact, the logical approach to most of the climbs takes a trail that leaves the Middle Fork Trail before reaching The Joint, and winds uphill above the crags. Climbers then descend to the second and third tiers to access the routes. The mass of routes are concentrated on the upper tiers, though some shorter crags lower on the buttress are also described. These small crags are best approached from below, via the Middle Fork Trail. Climbs are listed from left to right, starting on the Third Tier.

Third Tier

1. Sportsline 11c ★★

This is a bolted, right-facing corner on left end of ledge. Originally led on spasre gear, this route was bolted about ten years after the first ascent.

2. Unnamed 11b ★

This climb takes the face right of *Sportsline*. Look for a left-facing lieback/seam to start.

3. Willie's Wall, Pitch 2 10a ★

Continuation of *Willie's Wall* from Tier 2. Takes an obvious crack system past a bush to a small overhang, then moves left.

4. Willie's Wall, Direct Variation 10b ★★

This is the finger crack straight up at the end of *Willie's Wall*.

5. Megalomania 11a ★

This route takes a crack system to ¾ height, then traverses left about 10 feet. Continue up a left-facing corner to the top.

6. Black Water 7

This follows a left-facing corner in a black water streak. You can exit left or right, the right being easier.

Second Tier

7. The Chimney 5

At the extreme left-end of the second tier. Scramble up on a ledge, then around a corner into this non-appealing slot. Chances are, your will be the third ascent!

8. The Ramp 7 ★

This unique climb takes a left-trending ramp/crack system that ends in a slot. The squeeze chimney left is about 5.8. 50 feet

9. Good and Plenty 10a ★★

This is a right facing corner climb with some zig-zags. It sits just left of a diagonal black dike.

10. Willie's Wall, Pitch 1 10b ★★

Face climb starting on a "spike" boulder. 5 bolts to anchors at upper ledge. 50 feet

11. Instructor of the Future 13a ★★

This climb takes the face right of a broad, rounded arête in the middle of the cliff. 5 bolts. 50 feet

12. Willie's Corner 5 ★★

A low-angle corner with several cracks working up it. 50 feet

13. Lead Wall 9 ★

Climb a crack system in the middle of the face right of *Willie's Corner*. Pass a small roof, then step left to join *Willie's*. A direct finish takes the seams above through steeper ground (10b).

14. Hanging Corner 8

Start in a left-facing corner and then climb steeper cracks above, just left of a black streak.

15. Corner 6 ★

The climb starts just behind a big, leaning pillar. Climb the pillar, then follow a nice hand and fist crack to the top.

16. Arête 7

Follow seams up to a dihedral on an arête.

First Tier

Only one recorded climb breaks the first tier. This is the first pitch of Tom Hargis' three pitch ramble.

17. Hargis Route 11a ★★★

This is a three pitch affair that climbs the entire height of the Granite Buttress. Pitch on follows low-angle corners, ending on the Second Tier just below *Willie's Corner*. Move right to a pitch up the prow right of *Lead Wall*, ending at a bolted anchor on the Third Tier. Pitch three starts behind a large block, and takes a bolted face left of *Black Water*. Rappel route or walk off right.

Z-Crack Wall

This cliff is at the right end of the "First Tier" of the Granite Buttress. These cracks and corners were well-traveled in the 1960s and 1970s, but have seen little activity in recent years. The Z-Crack Wall is clearly visible from the Middle Fork Trail below the buttress, and is best approached by hiking up the trail rather than the traditional Granite Buttress approach.

18. Unnamed 8
This climb takes a right-facing chimney just right of a blank, clean wall. There is a large bush in the crack, but that doesn't tell you much...most of these routes have large bushes in them. Pass an overhang at the top by moving right. Have a nice grovel.

19. Unnamed 6
This climb takes a right-leaning, offset wide crack 10 feet right of a nice-looking arête. Ledges at the start give way to more strenuous climbing above. Gives an appreciation for how good most other climbs on Earth are.

20. Z Crack Overhang 9 ★
This is the best route on this cliff. A slightly-overhanging crack and face climb. After reaching the small ledge near the top, stay left to sustain the thrill.

21. Z Corner 8
This climb is in a major corner. Climb up to a ledge at 1/3 height (with a big bush on it), then up a right-facing crack above.

22. Z Crack 6 ★
Climb up a nice crack to a horizontal with blocks on it, move left 15 feet, up a crack to a ledge, then left again and up to the top.

Practice Wall ———————————————————

This wall sits just above the Middle Fork Trail. Approach it by wandering uphill just after passing a boulder that has a large overhang just above the trail. Most climbers don't ever climb here, but those who do usually top rope these 25-foot routes. Climbs are listed left-to-right. No photo.

23. Overlap Crack 9

24. Sapper Face 9

25. Sapper Corner 9

26. Sapper Crack 8

Andersonville ———————————————————

This crag is another 15 minutes up the Middle Fork Trail from the Granite Buttress. Continue past the falls cutoff, and stay right at the fork in the trail beyond. A series of switchbacks leads into some granite. Beyond, the terrain levels out and a large cliff can be found just right of the trail. There are several cracks and slabs on this wall, but only one recorded climb. If this route weren't awesome, there's no way I'd have wasted the time writing this paragraph.

27. The Lonely Town of Andersonville 12b ★★★ no photo
This is the overhanging hand-to-finger crack that splits the left side of the wall. Scramble to a small ledge to start. 60 feet

FOSSIL HILL

FOSSIL HILL

This wonderful crag sits on the high ridge south of Sinks Canyon (see photo in the Introduction). Fossil Hill is bighorn dolomite, but tends to have more edges than pockets. It also tends to be a little taller than most of the local cliffs. This cliff sits at a higher elevation than the Sinks, and is slightly cooler in the summer.

The first climbs at Fossil Hill were done in the summer of 1991 by Frank Dusl and friends. The first season here yielded over half the routes at the cliff. Over the following years, the "usual suspects" Greg Collins, Todd Skinner, Dave Doll, Steve Bechtel, and Paul Piana added to this wonderful crag. Now boasting more than 50 climbs, this is a nice respite from the heat of Sinks Canyon and the endless pocket-pulling of Wild Iris.

DRIVE TIME: 20 minutes from Lander

HIKE: 15 minutes uphill

SUN EXPOSURE: Sunny 11 a.m. to 5 p.m.

SEASON: Spring, Summer and Fall; access limited in Winter

LENGTH: 50 to 100 feet

FOSSIL HILL ROUTE COUNT by GRADE

5.10 : 6 — 5.11 : 12 — 5.12 : 20 — 5.13 : 6 — 5.14 : 1

GETTING THERE (Fossil Hill)

The switchbacks leading to Fossil Hill, above Bruce's Parking Area, are usually closed from mid-Nov. through May. Drive up Sinks Canyon past the Bruce's Parking Area (11.3 miles from downtown), and up the switchbacks until the first hill is crested (about 5 miles past Bruce's). At this point, the cliff will be visible to your left above a paved parking lot with a pit toilet..

APPROACH (Fossil Hill)

The climbers' trail heads east of the ATV scars, and is a faint footpath heading at an easy diagonal incline. Follow this trail past a barbed-wire fence, and eventually into forest below the cliff. **The trail hits the cliff at route 34.**

Routes 1 and 2 might be best accessed by walking straight uphill from the parking area, as they are quite removed from the bulk of the climbs.

FOSSIL HILL

Routes 1 & 2

Climbers' trail to the Main Cliff and the rest of the climbs

Routes are described left to right across the cliff; although the trail hits the cliff at route 34

1. The Swiss Indirect 11b
This route is at the prow of Fossil Hill, about 1/4 mile west of the main climbing.

2. The Dutch Directissimo 10c
Another route at the prow, no info.

3. Milk Bone 13a ★
Follows hard pockets up pretty orange wall 150 yards left of *Fossil Logic*. No photo. 5 bolts, 45 feet

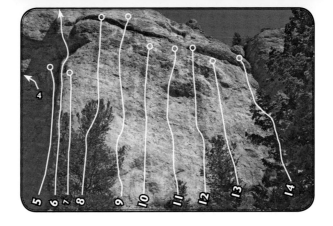

4. Project
The high bulge, anchors only.

5. Fossil Logic 11c ★★
Start climbing up big corner, then move right and out big wave wall on big holds. 70 feet

6. Hell Bent for the Horizon 12d ★★
Up pretty and steep west facing wall. 110 feet

7. Project Sound of Silence
The prow project.

8. Tremors 13a ★★
Hard long moves on crimps and monos. 70 feet

9. Unforgiven 12d ★
Continuously bouldery moves on some really thin holds. 70 feet

10. Channel Zero 11c ★★★
Enjoyable long moves up pretty streak. 65 feet

11. Household Chemicals 12b
Hard start to beautiful upper wall. 70 feet

12. Graboids 12a ★
Powerful moves low to fun bulge above. 70 feet

13. No Seats in Hell 11c ★★
Continuous climbing to a baffling crux. 70 feet

14. Furniture in Heaven 10a
Strange and filthy climbing. 60 feet

Routes
4 to 14

Routes
15 to 24

Routes
25 to 31

FOSSIL HILL

15. Highjackers 12c
Climb up seams and liebacks to hard moves. 60 feet

16. From Hell to Breakfast 12b
A pretty wall with hard long moves. 60 feet

17. Diamond Mouth 12c
Baffling crux after crux. Good climbing. 60 feet

18. Show Love 10d
Start in corner then go right and up face above. 65 feet

19. Project

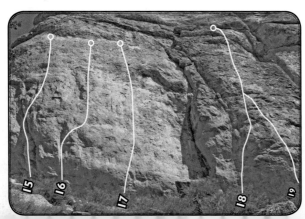

Routes
32 to 43

Routes
44 to 48

Routes
50 to 52

Fossil Hill

20. King of Fools 12b ★

Long and hard moves, crimps to high bulge. 80 feet

21. Queen of Spades 11d ★★

Crimpy start. Thin moves up vertical wall, then strenuous above roof to anchors. 80 feet

22. Project

Face behind tree

23. The Empty Quarter 11d

Starts up thin flake to good moves. A bit burly through the bulge. 85 feet

24. The Full Nickel 11b ★

Good climbing on varied rock. 85 feet

25. Merely Mortal 11a ★★

Begin in corner, then up vertical wall to anchors. 80 feet

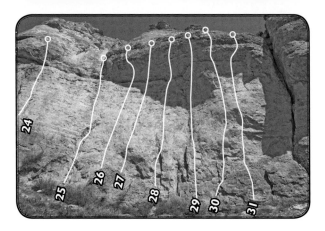

26. Vision of a Kiss 12b ★★
Fight through long moves on vertical rock to a really good bulge. 80 feet

27. Hips Like Cinderella 12c ★★★
One of the best. Hard low crux, then hard through high roof. 85 feet

28. The Saucy and the Brave 12c
Hard and weird low, great bulge high. 80 feet

29. Casual Entertainment 11c ★★★
Starts up big pillar, then up prow through bulges. 80 feet

30. Hang Fire 12a ★★★
Sustained difficulty and pump. Look for big hueco near bolt three. 80 feet

31.Tender Prey 12a ★★
Underclings and sidepulls lead to easier climbing above, then through tricky roof. 80 feet

32. Space Needle 12a ★★
Up crack in corner past tiny tree, then through two bulges. 70 feet

33. Two Ducks and an Angel 10b ★
Fun prow/corner route. 80 feet

34. Monster Match 13c ★★
Climb concave bulge to easy face above. 75 feet

35. Flying Roundhouse 12d ★★
Face to crack through bulge, then up headwall above. 11 bolts, 80 feet

36. Project
7 bolts, 60 feet

37. The Ol' Double Diamond 12b ★
Crack in corner, then traverse right and up prow. 70 feet

38. The Legend of Norm 12b ★★
Start same as *Double Diamond*, but traverse right around prow to good, long moves up steep wall. 70 feet

39. When the Cubans Hit the Floor 14a ★★
Up crack/corner to rail through roof, then up hard wall above. 60 feet

40. Project
Fibonacci Shimmer

41. The Righteous and The Wicked 13a ★★★
Underclings and crimps lead to easier climbing above. 90 feet

42. Unnamed 13b
Hard long moves.

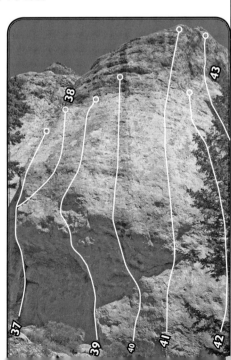

43. Fly Bones 13a ★
Just left of big corner up hard moves between good rests. 80 feet

44. Asian Rut aka Asian Orange 13c ★★
Beautiful orange streak on low-angle wall. 75 feet

45. Big in Japan 12a ★
Eleven bolts up face, then through prow. 80 feet

46. Maybe in the Next World 12a ★
Thin moves up slab, then through strenuous bulge. 80 feet

47. There Goes My Gun 11c ★★
Up seam then through cruxy bulge. 5.9 to first anchor. 75 feet

48. Vortec 10d
Hard slab to hard bulge. 65 feet

The trail drops away from the cliff near the route *Vortec*, **working its way below the huge jumble of boulders.**

49. Boom Stick 12a ★★

Short route on steep east wall of boulder near trail. No photo. 30 feet

50. Hero or Zero 11c ★★

Sustained difficulty to pumpy high crux. 80 feet

51. A Bullet for Mr. Ducky 10c ★★★

Great climbing up to water groove. 75 feet

52. Don't Call Me Shorty 11d ★

Shorter than the other routes on this wall, but thin. 50 feet

Scott Milton working *Orange for Anguish* (14c).
Photo © Bobby Model / M-11

BALDWIN CREEK

Baldwin Creek's main cliff is one of the most beautiful in America. The stone is very compact and features mostly pocket climbing on slightly overhanging walls. The climbs range in the 50 to 90 foot range, and most are equipped with clip anchors. This cliff was primarily developed during the 1993-1994 climbing seasons, with a small crew of dedicated climbers establishing some of the best routes in the entire Lander area.

DRIVE TIME: 45 minutes from Lander

HIKE: 30 minutes flat and downhill
You approach via the top of the crag

SUN EXPOSURE: Sunny until 7 p.m. most of the year

SEASON: Cool Summer evenings and Fall

LENGTH: 60 to 90 feet

BALDWIN ROUTE COUNT by GRADE

5.10 : 2 — **5.11** : 7 — **5.12** : 26 — **5.13** : 16— **5.14** : 1

GETTING THERE (Baldwin Creek)

From downtown Lander head west on Main toward the mountains. Just after 9th street, Main veers right, heading north to a traffic light. Take a left here, on Baldwin Creek Road. Continue west on Baldwin Creek Road. Follow this paved road for 5.5 miles, until the road turns to the south (left) and it is possible to continue west on an improved dirt road. After 0.9 miles, the road splits, with the left fork heading into a ranch and the right fork (Shoshone Lake Road) taking you north along a big red butte. Follow this road up several switchbacks to the crest of a small hill (about 5 miles).

At the top of this hill is a parking area popular with ATV riders. From here on up, the road continues up through meadows and aspens and is very rough in spots and requires a high-clearance vehicle.

After 10 to 15 minutes of slow going, near the crest of a hill, you'll pass a cattle guard and an "Entering Public Lands" sign. About 100 yards later, there is a clear area to park on the left, just before the road heads back downhill into a wooded drainage. This is the Baldwin Creek climbing area trailhead. 13.5 miles from Main Street in Lander. Subaru Outbacks can make it but the extra clearance of a truck is better.

APPROACH (Baldwin Creek)

From the parking area, walk west up the road for about 200 feet. There is a faint trail heading left (south) from here, and past a BLM trail kiosk that is 150 feet from the road. Follow a mostly flat path through a forest and over a small fence to an open meadow at the crest of a hill. This is a 12 to 15 minute walk so far.

Drop down the hill and follow faint switchbacks through a break in the cliff. Heading left as you go down the gully, you will find a footpath taking you down the cliff, back to the east. See photograph for Suicide Point.

The first climbs you reach break through the long, high horizontal roof, about 200 yards along the cliff from the descent gully. The bulk of the climbs, however, are another 3 to 5 minutes along. Look for the slightly overhanging black wall of *Brave Cowboy*, and the lone "shade tree" near *Amused to Death*.

The Climbs

Routes described from left to right as they are encountered.

1. Project
Through roof left of *Skyliner*.

2. Skyliner 13b ★★
11c to first anchor at top of flake. Break the huge roof above left of a seam. 100 feet

3. Magpies on an Afterbirth 12a
Gold shuts on slab, diagonals right. 75 feet

4. Two Projects
Right of gold shuts, direct line to end of *Magpies*.

5. Greased Lightning 12b
Starts below large bulge, climbs through bulge, then slightly left and up slab. 75 feet

6. Space Brigade 12a ★★
Up undercuts to steep wall. 95 feet

7. Swiss Miss 13a ★★
Less-than-vertical wall to anchors below square-cut roof. 90 feet

BALDWIN & SUICIDE CLOSURES

The road to Baldwin is typically closed from mid-November to June 1 of each year. Additionally, there are occasional raptor nesting closures that last until July 15 of each year. Please contact Wild Iris Mountain Sports in Lander at (307) 332-4541 about any current or potential closures.

8. White Lightning 10d ★★
Starts in crack, then up right into left-facing dihedral. 80 feet

9. Daybreaker 13b
Hard start leads to tricky climbing on rounded prow. 65 feet

10 . Troubleshooter 13a ★★
Steep face, shares anchors with *Mask*. 45 feet

11. Mask Without a Face 12a ★★★
Up steep climbing on good holds through bulge. 45 feet

12. Hair Trigger 12b

Start on underclings and sidepulls; then through roof on difficult moves. 70 feet

13. Where There's A Will, There's A Way 12c

Up through black roof, very bouldery. 70 feet

14. Pizza Hut Girl 12b ★★★

Up small arête, then right along lip of big roof. After rightward traverse; up on pumpy moves to anchor. 75 feet

15. Sideshow Bob 13b ★

Short, boulder-problem route right of the *Pizza Hut* roof. 40 feet

16. Beelzebubba 12a ★

Climb up tricky right-facing corner to easier ground. 65 feet

17. Break Like The Wind 11d ★

Climb seam to vertical face above. 65 feet

18. I Am A Fat Man 12c ★

Bulging wall. 65 feet

19. Black Jacques Serac 13a

Hard moves through bulge, easier up high. 70 feet

Tricia Stetson climbing *Brave Cowboy* (12a).
Photo © Bobby Model / M-11

20. Lucky Thirteen 12d
Tricky seam climbing to pumpy wall above. Technical. 80 feet

21. Mephisto 12c ★★
Long moves on generally good pockets. 80 feet

22. Western Family 12d
Another tricky seam climb. 75 feet

23. Surfer Rosa 12c ★
Climb up a pretty gold wall to high bulge. 80 feet

24. Little Pedro's Mexican Tidal Wave 12b ★★
Hard low move then left to pumpy headwall. 80 feet

25. Barbarossa 12b ★
Shares start with *Little Pedro*; then up right to hard steep climbing. 80 feet

26. Brave Cowboy 12a ★★★
Excellent route; starts in shallow left-facing corner, then climbs through hard steep wave. 80 feet

27. Très Amigos 12c ★★★
Hard low moves lead to a good rest, then a continuous hard headwall. 75 feet

28. Viva Hate 13d ★★
Through steep moves to easier climbing at top. 75 feet

29. The Power of One 13a ★★
Hard mono moves lead to a gold streak. 80 feet

30. Project No Cross, No Crown
31. Last Chance for a Slow Dance 12d ★
Climb up through steep wave, then right and up technical face above. 75 feet

32. Project
Straight up into *Last Chance* finish.

33. Burnout 13c
Black streak. Steep and continuous.

34. Graffiti Man 12d ★★
Starts on small prow; then up through small roofs along crack. 60 feet

35. Bittersweet 13c ★★
Very hard slab then through center of roofs. 70 feet

36. Supple Cowboy 13a ★
Climb left-facing corner to right side of roof; then up hard moves above. 60 feet

37. Cowboy This 13d ★★
This is the left-trending line of pockets on bullet-hard stone. Dusl's vision, Tilden's fingers. 65 feet

38. Project Wishing Well

39. Access Denied 13a ★★
Monos and long moves lead through a black wall. 65 feet

40. Project

41. State of Grace 12d ★
Very powerful moves up underclings and small pockets. 55 feet

42. Two Guys Names Festus 12d ★★★
Climb up long moves and thin pockets just left of the big tree. 65 feet

43. Amused to Death 12a ★★

Right of the big tree; climb up through left side of arch roof to spicy, yet easier, slab above. 70 feet

44. The Bravery of Being Out of Range 13a ★★

Climbs face to biggest part of roof; then up easier face above. 80 feet

45. Piston Hurricane 12b ★★★

Up good face to roof; through roof on good moves. 80 feet

46. TKO 12b ★★

Up right side of arch; then through roof. 80 feet

47. Rapid Fire 12b ★

Climb face just right of arch; continuous. 75 feet

48. Losing Streak 12b ★★★

A hard, beautiful grey streak. 80 feet

49. Voodoo Chile 11c

Starts on flake; up hard moves to easier slab above. 70 feet

50. Gimmie Shelter 11b ★★

Starts just left of large bush, climb up to undercling, over it, and up a good wall. 60 feet

51. Withering Heights 11a ★

Hard start just right of bush. Good pockets. 70 feet

52. One Trick Pony 11a
Poor and dirty climbing on a pretty-looking wall. 70 feet

53. Dinosaur Rock 10c ★★
Starts on grassy slope; climb on big pockets past small bulges. 60 feet

54. Ticket To Ride 11c ★
Good climbing on vertical wall left of orange roof/wave. 60 feet

55. Sunshine Superman 11b ★
Vertical, technical climbing. 65 feet

56. Can't Always Get What You Want 11d ★
Prow to slab. 65 feet

57. Rain of Gold 13b ★★★
Climb up arête to steep face above. 75 feet

58. Orange for Anguish 14c ★★
Up arête, then right and through center of steep wave. 85 feet

59. Project
Right side of wave.

60. A Bullet for Mr. Texas 13a ★★ no photo
200 yards further to the right. Nice route.

Todd Skinner on *Wind Drinker* **(12b).**
Photo © Bobby Model / M-11

SUICIDE POINT

Suicide is Lander's most alpine sport climbing area. This crag is the western-most end of the mighty Baldwin Creek Wall, but is provided as a separate chapter since it is approached from a different parking area and is some three miles west of the bulk of the Baldwin Creek climbs. The rock at Suicide is wind-weathered and is very angular. Many routes follow cracks, corners, and other distinct features. One of the 5.9s take natural gear so for this climb bring a few medium-sized cams. The rest are all bolted sport climbs on the most wild and beautiful crag around Lander.

See the previous Baldwin Creek chapter for more information on road closures (seasonal and for raptor nesting) affecting Suicide Point access.

DRIVE TIME: 50 minutes from Lander

HIKE: 5 minutes uphill

SUN EXPOSURE: Sunny 10 a.m. to dark

SEASON: Summer and Fall

LENGTH: 50 to 120 feet

SUICIDE POINT ROUTE COUNT by GRADE

5.9 : 2 — **5.10** : 1 — **5.11** : 3 — **5.12** : 6 — **5.13** : 2

The Climbs

A climbers' path leads up to the huge prow (*Wind Drinker*). All described climbs are within two minutes of this prow.

See the next page for approach details. Climbs are described left-to-right.

1. Hurricane Hannah 11b ★

Start up arête below *Wind Drinker* (the VERY obvious prow), then move left around corner to steep face. This climb was done by Amy and Todd Skinner the summer after their first daughter, Hannah, was born. 80 feet

2. Wind Drinker 12b ★★★

Up easy arête to anchor (5.6), then out "hatchet blade" prow. See photo in the Introduction. 70 feet

GETTING THERE (Suicide Point)

Follow the directions getting to the Baldwin Creek trailhead. From there, the road flattens out and then begins climbing once you reach the bottom of the drainage. Just over 1 mile past Baldwin's parking, you'll begin driving through open meadows and should be able to see the dramatic prow of Suicide Point on the ridge to your left. Turn left toward this cliff on an obvious two-track road, and drive up to a nice parking area on the ridge below the cliffs. A faint trail leads to the base of the climbs.

3. Suicide King 12c ★★★
Easy face climbing right of arête leads to long pulls up overhanging rock. 80 feet

4. Storm Chaser 11d ★
Starts in crack, then up steeper face above. Be careful to avoid climbing right to the *Weeping Wrist* anchors. 80 feet

5. Weeping Wrist 11b
Thin face through bulge to anchor in alcove. 65 feet

6. A Cry for Help 10c
Up slab to horizontal, then up short steep wall. Bolted by Dave Brinda way back in 1991 and then abandoned for the "more accessible" climbs of Baldwin Creek. 55 feet

7. Blue Steel 11d ★
This climb follows the vertical face to a short overhanging section, 10 feet left of *Flowers for a Dead Man*. 60 feet

8. Flowers for a Dead Man 13b
Up center of steep face. 60 feet

9. Painless 9 ★★
Climbs the steep offwidth corner. Fun. Lilygren had a great habit of rolling in and snagging the classics at every new crag. 60 feet

10. Nickel Winchester 12b ★★
Up edgy face, finishing below the roof. 60 feet

11. Apocalyptic Lapse Rate 9
Climbs the dihedral with natural and fixed protection. Bring cams to 2". 80 feet

12. Golden Ulric 12c ★★
Starts in corner, then out steep wall and through bulging rock above. 100 feet

See the Baldwin Creek chapter for more information on road closures (seasonal and for raptor nesting) affecting Suicide & Baldwin.

Suicide Point at upper left-hand skyline. Baldwin Creek on the right (approach trail marked). This commanding cliff extends another two miles off to the right

13. Silver Nimschkie 13b ★★

Underclings through bulge, then up through thin pockets. 80 feet

14. Stormbringer 12d ★★★

Up corner to anchor (5.9), then out 20 foot horizontal roof. 75 feet

15. Cloudwalker 12b ★★

This route shares the long corner start of *Stormbringer*, then breaks right out a slightly easier section of the roof. 75 feet

16. Projects

Two projects 100 feet right of *Cloudwalker*.

Suicide Point Overview

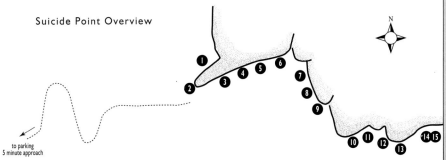

to parking
5 minute approach

FIRST ASCENTS by ROUTE

Crowheart, Paul Piana, 2002
Cutthroat, Paul Piana, 2000
C'est Fini, Bob Branscomb, 2007
D.O.A. Mike Collins, 1986
D.O.E. Greg Collins, 1986
Dag Nab It, Rob Hess, 1990
Dances with Wolves, Shane Petro, 1991
Dancing With Godzilla, Michael Lindsey, 1993
Dare, Unknown, 1980s
Darksides, Rob Hess, 1989
Daybreaker, Todd Skinner, 1994
Dead Bird Crack, Unknown 1970s
Deadman's Reach, Steve Bechtel, 2009
Dealer Calls, BJ Tilden, 2009
Dennis and Jacques' Excellent Adventure,
D VanDenbos, J Rutschmann, 1997
Devil Lock, Vance White, 2008
Devilution, Vance White, 2011
Dewalt's Challenge, Trey Warren, 1997
Diamond Mouth, Paul Piana, 2000
Diamonds and Rain, Eric Hörst, 1992
Diemos, Tom Hargis, 2001
Digital Stimulation, Jeff Leafgreen, 2000
Dime Time, Greg Collins, 1992
Dinosaur Rock, Mike Lindsey, 1994
Dirt Bag, John Warning, 1996
Dirty Sally, Jeremy Rowan, 2009
Divine Intervention, Frank Dusl, 1994
Dogfight at the OK Corral,
Pete Delannoy, 1992
Doggin' Dude, Jeff Leafgreen, 1998
Dogs of War, Frank Dusl, 1992
Dogtown, Vance White, 2007
Doll Face, Paul Piana, 2004
Doll Parts, Paul Piana, 1996
Don Ho, Todd Skinner, 2002
Don't Bring Your Guns to Town,
John Hennings, 2006
Don't Call Me Shorty, Dave Doll, 2000
Don't Paint Your Wagon, Craig Reason, 1991
Dorsal, Eric Sawyer, 1988
Dr. Endeavor, Unknown
Dreaming the Rasta Bus,
Bob Branscomb, 2010
Dreaming the Rasta Bus, Bob Branscomb, 2010
Driller's Delight, Greg Collins, 1989
Drinking Dry Clouds, John Hennings, 2006
Drug Enemy, Greg Collins, 1997
Drugstore Cowboy, Pete Delannoy, 1992
Duck Soup, Dave Doll, 1999
Dumb Bunnies, Greg Collins, Larry Berger, 1980
Dutch Rudder, Jeremy Rowan, 2009

Dynamitic, Rick Thompson, 2000
EZ Up, Unknown, 1990s
Eagle Dance, Greg Collins, 1984
Earth A.D., Vance White, 2007
Easy Ridin', Diedre Burton, 1996
Ego Tripper, Unknown
El Toro, Unknown, 1993
Electric Fence, Paul Piana, 2001
Elmo's Fish, Heidi Badaracco, 2000
Empire, Tom Rangitsch, 2008
Endeavor to Persevere, Craig Reason, 1991
Endeavor to Stab Bush, Leif Gasch, 2005
Eros, Tom Hargis, 2001
Even Cowgirls get the Blues,
Laurie Medina, 1990
Every Gun Sings Its Own Song,
Pete Delannoy, 1992
Ewenanimity, Rick Thompson, 2000
Exile on Main Street, Bob Branscomb, 1993
Exodus, Vance White, 2006
Face Dancer, Joe Desimone, 1993
Fallen Idol, Greg Collins, 1990
Fat Back, Greg Collins, Reave Castenholz, 1980
Fat Boys Skip School, Mike Lindsey, 1994
Fear and Loathing, Jason Stephens, Scott
Howard, 2007
Fear of Flying, S Fisher, Randy Cerf, 1978
Fine Dining, Greg Collins, 1998
Finish Your Homework, Kirk Billings, 1996 (to first
anchors). Jim Ratz, 1999 (complete route)
Firecracker Kid, Tim Rawson, 1984
First Responder, Ty Mack, 2004
Fist Full of Quickdraws, Sam Lightner, 1991
Five Year Plan, Eric Sawyer, 1990
Fizzle Doubt, Paul Piana, 2002
Flowers For a Dead Man, Todd Skinner, 1998
Fly Bones, Paul Piana, 2001
Flying Roundhouse, Steve Bechtel, 2000
Fossil Logic, Heidi Badaracco, 2000
Foundation, Tom Rangitsch, 2008
Four Dead Aliens, Greg Collins, Tom Daughton, 1984
Franklin's Tower, Greg Collins, George Flam, 1981
Freak Factor, Rick & John Horn, 1967
French Blow, Jesse Brown, 2011
Friday the 13th, Mike Collins 1986
Friend or Faux, Rick Thompson, 2000
From Hell to Breakfast, Paul Piana, 2000
Full Circle, Matt Wendling, 2008
Full Irations, Greg Collins, 1999
Full Moon, Keith Lennard, 1990
Full Tilt, Greg Collins, 1989
Fun Planet, Georgie Stanley, 1992

Rodeo Free Europe, Jason Campbell, 1998
Rokai Corner, Vance White, 2007
Roll in the Hay, Pat Thompson, 1997
Royal Edge, Geoff Heath, Jeb Schenck, 1974
Rubber Soul, Jim Ratz, 1997
Ruby Shooter, Heidi Badaracco, 1992
Ryobi Jr., Pat Perrin, 1991
Ryobi Ranger, Pat Perrin, 1991
Ryobi Rustler, Pat Perrin, 1991
Ryobi Wrangler, Pat Perrin, 1991
Sacagawea, Elaine Chandler, 1990
Saddle Up, Unknown, 1990s
Saddled Dreams, Jeremy Rowan, 2009
Salsa for the Sole, Rick Thompson, 2000
Sam I Am, Steve Bechtel, 2008
Samsara, Kirk Billings, 2002
Sand Digger, Hassan Saab, 1991
Sandman, Jim Ratz, 1995
Sandy But Dandy Direct, T Walter, J Hauf, 1986
Sandy But Dandy, T Walter, M Miller, 1986
Santa Cleopatra, Heidi Badaracco, 1994
Sapper Corner, Unknown
Sapper Crack, Unknown
Sapper Face, Unknown
Saucerful of Secrets, Bob Branscomb, 1996
Savages, Greg Collins, 1989
Save A Prayer For Lefty, Todd Skinner, 2004
Say Hello to Geronimo, Bob Branscomb, 1994
ScAiry, Eric Sawyer, 1994
Scary Canary, Unknown, 2004
Screaming Trees, Bob Branscomb, 1991
Scud Alert, Greg Collins, 1990
Searching for Jose Cuervo, Craig Reason, 1991
Second Hand Nova, Jeff Leafgreen, 1999
Second Helping, Bob Branscomb, 2008
Secret Slab, Bob Branscomb, 1996
Sentinel Chimney, R Cerf, G Heath, B Brudigam, 1976
Sentinel Crack Direct, Rob Hess ,1990
Sentinel Cracks, John Hauf, 1984
Shades, Frank Dusl, 1992
Shadowline, Bob Branscomb, 2004
Shao Lin Degree, BJ Tilden, 2008
Shao Lin ShadowBoxing, Geoff Sluyter? 1999
Sharps 50, Alf Randell, 2006
Sheepeater, Todd Skinner, 2006
Shortie Sortie, Greg Collins, 1990
Show Love, Greg Collins, 2000
Sideshow Bob, Todd Skinner, 1994
Sign of the Times, Frank Dusl, 1992
Silver Nimschkie, Todd Skinner, 1998
Silverbelly, Paul Piana, 1996

Sister Ray, Greg Collins, 1991
Skinny Fat Man, Unknown, 1992
Skyliner, Todd Skinner, 1994
Slapping Leather, John Gogas, 1991
Slave to History, Bob Branscomb, 2007
Slave, Unknown, 1990s
Sleeping Thunder, Paul Piana, 1993
Slick Fifty, Steve Bechtel, 2006
Slippery People, Porter Jarrard, 1992
Smell My Finger, Mark Howe, 2002
Smirk, John Hennings, 2006
Smoke Shapes, Matt Lund, 1998
Snap Back Relax, Greg Collins, 2000
Soft Option, Steve Bechtel, 2006
Software, Paul Piana, 1996
Some Like Another Chance, Bob Branscomb, 2010
Sorta Maybe Kinda Wild, Bob Branscomb, 1996
Sorting Hat Left, Bob Branscomb, 2004
Sorting Hat Right, Bob Branscomb, 2004
Soul Finger, Steve Bechtel, 2006
Soup Sandwich, Steve Bechtel, 2006
Southpaw, Tom Hargis, 2000
Space Brigade, BJ Tilden, 2006
Space Needle, Heidi Badaracco, 2000
Spaghetti Western, Pete Delannoy, 1991
Spank the Monkey, Eric Ming, 1995
Spent Rods, Gary Wilmot, 1992
Spike n' Vein, Greg Collins, 1994
Spinal Tap, Dennis VanDenbos, 1999
Spook Eyes, Paul Piana, 1999
Spooky Tooth, Bob Branscomb, 1996
Sportsline, Greg Collins, 1988
Spragglepuss, Vance White, 1999
Spurs Equal Velocity, Heidi Badaracco, 1992
Stacked Deck, Pete Delannoy, 1992
Stairway to Heaven, Jesse Brown, 2010
Standard Route, G Heath, R Rosenthal, J Laden, 1966
Standard Start, Geoff Heath,1967
State of Grace, Frank Dusl, 1993
Steel Pulse, Vance White, 2010
Stiff Upper Lip, John Hennings, 2006
Stirrup Trouble, Unknown, 1992
Stone Ranger, Leif Gasch, 2006
Stone Seed, Greg Collins, 1995
Storm Chaser, Todd Skinner, 1996
Storm Warning, Greg Collins, 1998
Storm of the Century, Mike Lindsey, 1996
Stormbringer, Steve Petro, 1998
Straight Outta Hudson, Steve Bechtel, 2005
Straight Up Crew, Greg Collins, 1996
Straight, No Chaser, Ed Delong, 1992
Stronger Than Reason, Matt Lund, 1997

ROUTE INDEX by GRADE

5.11c

5.11d

5.13a

5.13b

Please help us out and send in any of the following: errors or typos you find in this book; broken holds; to call bullshit on a sandbag; find a route line in the wrong place: or anything else you think might be useful. If you have established a new route, it is highly encouraged to let us know. This is not a canned plea for help. In reality, unsolicited updates are about as common as a Democrat winning a Wyoming Presidental election.

This makes it very time consuming and difficult to stay on top with accurate and updated information. The information that is most useful typically comes from the average yet passionate climbers that are out there weekend after weekend, hanging at the base and around the campfire with other core climbers, epicking on some obscure testpiece, or simply doing an easy standard for their umpteenth time.

Most people assume someone else has already reported the mistakes or submitted updates on a new line of bolts that appeared since last fall. It just ain't so. So *PLEASE*, no matter how random or insignificant any piece of information or photo may seem, every single bit helps. If there is something about this book you don't like, this is your chance to help us improve. An easy way to recieve a free copy of the next updated and expanded edition is if we publish your killer action shot. Future editions will be so much better for it and if nothing else, it will improve our ability to get them completed and available that much quicker. Thanks in advance.

Please send to:

elemental
climbing

Elemental Training Center
134 Lincoln
Lander, WY 82520
or email to:
steve@elementaltraining.com

LOWER OFF A WORN OUT ANCHOR?
FIND A BOLT THAT NEEDS REPLACING?

Contact the author (at the above Lander address) or the staff at Wild Iris Mountain Sports. Wild Iris and local climbers do, from time to time, have money, equipment and manpower available to support the replacement of bolts and anchors.

See page 16 for more details.